SKILL-STREAM-ING THE ADOLES-CENT

A STRUCTURED LEARNING APPROACH TO TEACHING PROSOCIAL SKILLS

Arnold P. Goldstein • Robert P. Sprafkin
N. Jane Gershaw • Paul Klein

RESEARCH PRESS COMPANY
2612 North Mattis Avenue
Champaign, Illinois 61821

D0454522

To our dear friend, the late Gilda Gold, whose work with troubled youngsters always reflected both special sensitivity and deep understanding.

And to our own youngsters, Susan and Cindy Goldstein, Jeff, Neal, and Noah Sprafkin, and Eric and Jason Klein, who have been our most candid reviewers and special sources of inspiration.

CONTENTS

FOREWORD

Schools are increasingly burdened with the responsibility of training young people not only in basic academic skills but also in coping with complex social and personal problems. It is all too tempting to respond to external pressures by focusing attention on problem behaviors and on classroom disruptions and to view youngsters' nonconstructive or nonconforming actions as obstacles to the achievement of the educational objectives prescribed by syllabi, directives, and laws. Recently, educators and counselors have begun to realize that the solutions to many of these problems may lie in concentrated efforts to build up the strengths and potentials of troublesome and troubled young people rather than in disciplinary or remedial action. First, constructive participation in the educational process requires some skills in dealing with the environment in which learning takes place. Second, the student must expect that he can achieve the objectives. Simple methods for teacher control of the classroom do not necessarily yield greater enthusiasm for learning.

In psychological approaches this realization has meant a shift from a focus on disruptive classroom behaviors to an emphasis on skill building. Public sentiment now appears to be more ready to accept the idea that children who are difficult to handle in school do not merely need help in learning to be quiet and docile but instead need to be helped to actively develop their capabilities as fully as possible. This book is an excellent example of this approach. The authors assume that deficiencies in social and planning skills and in abilities to deal with stress, feelings, and aggression represent major sources of conflict with peers, school teachers, and authorities. Increased competence in these areas can pave the way for a better education. The authors focus their attention on those adolescents who need remedial training before they can benefit from regular educational experiences and who are poorly prepared to deal with many social demands made on them. Such an approach does not ask what mischief youngsters can cause. It tries, instead, to help them develop coping skills and confidence in their own abilities to resolve conflicts so that they can benefit from education. The authors of this book offer a carefully planned and experimentally supported program that should go far in helping teachers, psychologists, counselors, and other trainers to achieve these goals.

The purpose of the program is to facilitate the education of adolescents who show some deficits in functioning in the "least restrictive environment" in school systems, as described in Public Law 94-142. Beyond that, the procedures should help trainers to maximize the potentials of the skill-deficient or handicapped adolescent for normal functioning in the community. Finally, such remedial programs should enhance the youngster's competence in dealing with interpersonal conflicts, increase his self-esteem, and indirectly contribute to a classroom atmosphere in which more attention can be given to subjects than to disruptive behavior or peer conflict.

Individually the authors have brought different skills to the creation of this book, and together they have integrated these skills to produce a program that draws on psychological and educational techniques. What has impressed me most is that the book offers a clear, practical guide to the trainer with specific examples of the general rules, almost in the form of a training manual. At the same time, readers are also acquainted with the major principles of Structured Learning theory on which the methods are based, so that they can apply the procedures, not in simple cookbook fashion, but with an understanding of the underlying theory and rationale. This broad base is supported by extensive research on Structured Learning methods with diverse target populations and the authors' combined experiences as educators, clinicians, and researchers.

There is a universal disadvantage in the use of any standardized procedure and group method. No youngster is similar in his behavior pattern and developmental history to any other adolescent. The authors are aware that individual variations must be taken into account to use a program competently and responsibly. Their concept of prescriptive intervention fits very well the belief that an individual analysis of a person's strengths and weaknesses is critical in order to match the youngster's needs with those portions of the program that are best suited to meet them. Effectiveness of the program depends on its appropriateness for a specific person in a particular setting. Therefore, the authors supplement the structuring of the training and description of the methods with a detailed discussion of the selection and grouping of the youngsters. Procedures for assessing individual skill repertoires and deficits are described and materials are provided to develop behavioral objectives relevant to particular adolescents. Such information permits grouping of youngsters so that identified skill deficits rather than identified problems, diagnostic labels, or subjective impressions guide the adolescent's assignment to groups.

No single book can offer all the information needed to conduct a full remedial program for youngsters in all settings. This book is unique because it provides a blend of practical and conceptual information sufficient to let trainers know what to do, how to do it, why to do it, and with whom to do it. It should reassure trainers who are faced with the difficult problem of ''mainstreaming'' that, indeed, much can be accomplished by careful and systematic use of Structured Learning principles.

F. H. Kanfer
University of Illinois
Champaign, Illinois
May 1979

ACKNOWLEDGEMENTS

A book such as this has several roots. Among these are the many teachers and others we trained as Structured Learning group leaders and from whom we learned so much in the process. The youngsters who made up the skill-training groups led by these trainers, as well as those in groups which we ourselves have led, have time and again had much to teach us in turn. Our graduate students, in both their research as well as in less formal interactions concerning the skill-training domain, have provided us with many fertile insights and intriguing leads. And our colleagues at Syracuse University, the Veterans Administration, and the Syracuse School District have been consistent sources of warm support and encouragement. Our sincerest appreciation to them all.

CHAPTER 1

A Prescriptive Introduction

"Fuck you," shouted Willie, and he shoved Mr. Osborne hard, up against the blackboard. "If you tell the principal me and Henry was fighting, I'll get suspended again. You just keep your fuckin' mouth shut." Willie loosened his hold on his shaken teacher's shirt, glared at him, and then spun around and returned to his seat.

In the school cafeteria, Betty sat alone quietly and ate her lunch as fast as possible so she could leave. She approached no one, spoke to no one, looked at no one. She tried to make herself small, invisible. She was sure others were watching her, thinking how ugly she looked. Mostly, she just wanted to cry.

John's behavior in school is quite typical for a six-year-old. He asks for help very often, pays attention only for short stretches, complains a lot, whines, daydreams much of the time. But John isn't six years old; he is eleven.

We have written this book out of concern for youngsters like Willie, Betty, and John. The first meets life challenges with aggression; the second withdraws; and the third responds, but with immature and inadequate behaviors. All three are skill deficient. They lack or are weak in the necessary skills and behaviors that all people need to lead effective and satisfying personal and interpersonal lives. This book's major focus is skill deficiency and its remediation through a skill training approach called Structured Learning. Structured Learning is explicitly designed to teach adolescents social skills, planning skills, skills for dealing with feelings, skill alternatives to aggression, and skills for responding effectively to stress. In this chapter, we will fully describe the youngsters who may be con-

1

sidered likely targets for such skill training and will briefly consider the array of other treatment and correctional approaches that have been employed thus far with such skill-deficient adolescents.

THE SKILL-DEFICIENT ADOLESCENT

How can skill-deficient youngsters best be described? A number of diverse attempts have been undertaken to develop classification systems which adequately describe children and adolescents exhibiting behavior disorders. Prior to 1966, 24 such systems had been proposed (Group for the Advancement of Psychiatry, 1966). Unfortunately, most of these systems essentially lacked evidence of sufficient reliability or evidence that they related meaningfully to decisions about the types of remedial treatment recommended. The Group for the Advancement of Psychiatry's (1966) own classification system made some beginning strides at dealing with these chronic deficiencies, but it still was inadequate. A truly useful system of classifying behavior disorders did not appear until multivariate statistical techniques and sophisticated computer technology were developed. With this new technology, recent investigators have been able to make use of very diverse types of information drawn from a broad range of behaviorally disordered adolescents. In this regard, Quay, Peterson, and their colleagues have used observational behavior ratings by teachers, parents, clinic staff, and correctional workers; case history materials; the responses of adolescents themselves to personality testing, and other types of information—all obtained from and about adolescents in public schools, child guidance clinics, institutions for delinquents, and mental hospitals. Using multivariate statistical techniques on these bodies of information, a three-category classification pattern has emerged. These three categories are aggression, withdrawal, and immaturity, and they account for the vast majority of behaviors typically included under the term *behavior disorders.* Although the particular classification system proposed by Quay and his co-workers will be described in this chapter, it is important to note that the same patterns found by these researchers have emerged consistently in other equally sophisticated classification efforts (Achenbach, 1966; Achenbach & Edelbrock, 1978; Brady, 1970; Hewitt & Jenkins, 1946; Patterson & Anderson, 1964; Peterson, Quay, & Tiffany, 1961; Ross, Lacey, & Parton, 1965).

Aggression

Quay (1966) comments:

> Almost without exception multivariate statistical studies of problem be-
> haviors . . . reveal the presence of a pattern involving aggressive behav-
> ior, both verbal and physical, associated with poor interpersonal relation-
> ships with both adults and peers. This pattern has received a variety of
> labels: e.g., unsocialized aggressive (Hewitt & Jenkins, 1946); conduct
> problem (Peterson et al., 1961; Quay & Quay, 1965); aggressive (Pat-
> terson & Anderson, 1964); unsocialized psychopath (Quay, 1964); psy-
> chopathic delinquency (Peterson, Quay, & Cameron, 1959); antisocial
> aggressiveness and sadistic aggressiveness (Dreger et al., 1964); and
> externalizing (Achenbach, 1966). (p. 9)

This classification reflects such specific behaviors as fighting, disruptiveness, destructiveness, profanity, irritability, quarrelsomeness,
defiance of authority, irresponsibility, high levels of attention-
seeking behavior, and low levels of guilt feelings. In Quay's research,
youngsters in this category typically answer affirmatively to such
questionnaire items as:

> I do what I want to whether anybody likes it or not.
> The only way to settle anything is to lick the guy.
> If you don't have enough to live on, it's OK to steal.
> It's dumb to trust other people.
> I'm too tough a guy to get along with most kids.

Quay (1966) observes that the essence of this pattern is an active
antisocial aggressiveness that inevitably results in conflict with
parents, peers, and social institutions. Children and adolescents
whose behavior reflects this pattern in the extreme are likely to be in
such difficulty as to be involved in the courts and institutions for
delinquents.

Withdrawal

The behavior disorder pattern characterized by withdrawal has been
variously labeled overinhibited (Hewitt & Jenkins, 1946), personality problem (Peterson et al., 1961), disturbed neurotic (Quay,
1964), internalizing (Achenbach, 1966), and withdrawn (Patterson
& Anderson, 1964; Ross, Lacey, & Parton, 1965). Quay (1966)
describes this pattern further.

These behaviors, attitudes, and feelings clearly involve a different pattern of social interaction than do those comprising conduct disorder; they generally imply withdrawal instead of attack. In marked contrast to the characteristics of conduct disorder are such traits as feelings of distress, fear, anxiety, physical complaints, and open and expressed unhappiness. It is within this pattern that the child who is clinically labeled as an anxiety neurotic or as phobic will be found. (p. 11)

The behavior disorder pattern characterized by withdrawal is also often marked by depression, feelings of inferiority, self-consciousness, shyness, anxiety, hypersensitivity, seclusiveness, and timidity.

Immaturity

Immaturity, the third prominent class of adolescent behavior disorders, has been identified in samples of adolescents studied in public schools, child guidance clinics, and institutions for delinquents. Behaviors included in the immaturity pattern include short attention span, clumsiness, preference for younger playmates, passivity, daydreaming, and incompetence. This pattern represents a persistence of behaviors that were largely age-appropriate earlier in the youngster's development but which have become inappropriate in view of his current age and society's expectations of the adolescent.

Quay's (1966) reflections on the three patterns of behavior disorders are most relevant to our skill deficiency focus. He comments:

The characteristics of the three . . . patterns may all be said to be clearly maladaptive either from the social or individual viewpoint. Extremes of such behaviors are at variance with either the expectations of self, parents, or educational and other social institutions. . . . Each of the previous patterns also involves interpersonal alienation with peers, attack in the case of conduct disorders, withdrawal in the case of personality disorders, or lack of engagement in the case of immaturity. (pp. 13-14)

These descriptions of the aggressive, withdrawn, or immature adolescent focus on what each youngster does. But from a skill-deficiency viewpoint it is also profitable to examine what each youngster does not do. Thus, the aggressive adolescent often is not only proficient in fighting, disruptiveness, destructiveness, and similar antisocial skills, but may also be deficient in such prosocial skills as self-control, negotiation, asking permission, avoiding trouble with others, understanding the feelings of others, and dealing with someone else's anger. The withdrawn youngster, in an analogous manner, may lack proficiency in such prosocial skills as having a conversation, joining in, dealing with fear, decision making, dealing with being left out, responding to persuasion, and dealing with contradictory messages. This kind of youngster also lacks the skills relevant to expressing or receiving apologies, complaints, or instructions. The parallel skill deficiency pattern for the immature adolescent typically may involve a lack of competence in sharing, responding to teasing, responding to failure, dealing with group pressure, goal setting, and concentration. The prosocial skills listed here are a brief sampling of the target skills that form the major focus of Structured Learning.

Developmental Hurdles

We have proposed that behaviorally disordered youngsters may be reliably categorized in terms of three major types. Each type may be described in terms of both the presence of a repertoire of dysfunctional and often antisocial behavior and of the absence of a repertoire of prosocial or developmentally appropriate behaviors. It is our belief that a training program oriented toward the explicit teaching of prosocial skills can remediate many of these skill deficits. Desirable, functional skills missing from an individual's behavioral repertoire can be taught successfully. However, it is not only the aggressive, withdrawn, or immature youngster who may benefit from such training. Many other adolescents who are less likely to come to the attention of school, clinic, or institution personnel can also benefit from skill-training efforts. Manster (1977), in his book *Adolescent Development and Life Tasks,* describes the sequence of life tasks that all adolescents must master. In school, at work, in the community, with peers, family, authority figures—in all of these settings the developing adolescent meets, must cope with, and master an increasingly complex series of personal and interpersonal life tasks. Love, sex, and peer relationships are likely to require social skills (e.g., having a conversation, listening, joining in), skills for dealing with feelings (e.g., dealing with fear, expressing affection, understanding the feelings of others), and skills useful for dealing with stress (e.g., dealing with embarrassment, preparing for a stressful conversation, responding to failure). School-related tasks demand proficiency at yet other skills, in particular, planning skills (e.g., goal setting, gathering information, decision making). School settings also require daily success at tasks involving both peers (e.g., dealing with group pressure) and authority figures (e.g., following instructions). Similarly, work settings are also multifaceted in their task demands and, hence, in their requisite skills, especially those requiring planning and stress management. For many youngsters, whether in school, at work, or elsewhere, the skill demands placed on them will frequently involve the ability to deal satisfactorily with aggression, either their own or someone else's. In these instances, skills to be mastered may include self-control, negotiation, and dealing with group pressure.

The developmental tasks we have described are not easily mastered, and efforts to aid their progression appear to be worthwhile. It is in this sense that the "average" adolescent, experiencing the need for assistance over certain developmental hurdles, is also a potential target trainee for the approach described in this book.

TREATMENT AND TRAINING APPROACHES

A number of diverse approaches exist for the training, treatment, and rehabilitation of aggressive, withdrawn, immature, and other seriously skill-deficient youngsters. These include such putative correctional rehabilitative procedures as incarceration and probation, an array of individual and group psychotherapies, a series of newer behavioral techniques designed to alter overt maladaptive or antisocial behavior by the management of reward contingencies, and, very recently, certain psychoeducational therapies that usually attempt to increase the adolescent's proficiency in prosocial skills, thus decreasing reliance on antisocial behaviors. Each of these approaches has its proponents and opponents. For each there are testimonials, critiques, and, in some instances, research studies supporting its value.

The view in this text regarding these correctional, rehabilitative, counseling, psychotherapeutic, behavioral, and psychoeducational procedures is prescriptive. By this we mean that none of them may be viewed as "good" or "bad" or "effective" or "ineffective" in any absolute sense. The recent history of psychotherapy offers an example. In the 1950s, when research on the effectiveness of psychotherapy was just beginning, investigators asked, "Does treatment A work?" or "Is treatment A better than treatment B?" But

answers to such questions, even when positive, proved to be virtu-
ally useless. Little or no information was provided by answers to
such global questions either about how to improve the effectiveness
of the particular treatment (since it was studied as a whole, with no
attention to its separate components) or how to use the research
findings to help the individual person (because only group effects
were studied).

In response to such shortcomings, and the awareness that as yet
none of our treatments can be sufficiently powerful to help all or almost all types of people, clinicians and researchers have begun to
ask, ''Which type of patient, meeting with which type of therapist,
for which type of treatment, will yield which outcome?'' This question reflects a prescriptive view of the helping enterprise. It attempts
to match patients, therapists, and treatments so that the likelihood of
a beneficial outcome is maximized. This prescriptive viewpoint has
been discussed in considerable detail elsewhere (Goldstein, 1978;
Goldstein & Stein, 1976).

In 1974, Martinson published an article titled ''What Works?'',
a review of diverse efforts to alter the deviant behavior of juvenile offenders. Research on the treatments and correctional efforts examined by Martinson focused on a large number of diverse intervention
procedures. His conclusion was unequivocal: ''With few and iso-
lated exceptions, the rehabilitative efforts that have been reported so
far have had no appreciable effect on recidivism'' (p. 25). Palmer
(1975) has shown, however, that this singularly negative conclusion
rests on Martinson's reliance on what we have called the ''one true
light assumption'' (Goldstein & Stein, 1976). This assumption, the
antithesis of a prescriptive viewpoint, holds that specific treatments
are sufficiently powerful to override substantial individual differences and aid heterogeneous groups of patients. Research in all fields
of psychotherapy has shown the one true light assumption to be
erroneous (Goldstein, 1978; Goldstein & Stein, 1976), and Palmer
(1976) has shown it to be especially in error with regard to aggressive and delinquent adolescents. Palmer reviewed the data from
which Martinson drew his ''nothing works'' conclusion and
pointed out that in each of the dozens of studies concerned, there
were homogeneous subsamples of adolescents for whom the given
treatments under study had worked. Martinson's error was that he

had been unresponsive to the fact that when homogeneous subsamples are combined to form a heterogeneous full sample, the various positive, negative, and no-change treatment outcome effects of the subsamples cancel each other out. The result is that the full sample appears no different than an untreated group. But when smaller, more homogeneous subsamples are examined separately, many treatments do work. The task then is not to continue the futile pursuit of the so-called one true light—the one treatment that works for all—but, instead, to discern which treatments administered by which treaters work for whom, and for whom they do not.*

Incarceration

It is one thing to espouse a prescriptive clinical strategy regarding the treatment of disturbed and disturbing adolescents, but quite another to implement such a strategy. Our state of prescriptive knowledge is primitive. Most investigators and correctional practitioners, for example, view incarceration as the least desirable alternative treatment for juvenile offenders. "Locking them up" as a correctional treatment is seen as often leading to more and not less eventual antisocial behavior. Yet in almost every instance, holders of this essentially anti-incarceration viewpoint simultaneously acknowledge, directly or by implication, that there likely is a subsample of offenders that has yet to be specified (probably characterized chiefly by a high prior rate of recidivism) for whom incarceration may well be the optimal intervention (Achenbach, 1974; Bailey, 1966; Empey, 1969; Kassenbaum, Ward, & Wilner, 1972; McClintock, 1961; Robinson & Smith, 1976).

Probation

Probation, too, has its champions as a differentially offered treatment. Evidence exists that it may be an appropriate intervention for

---

*Those involved in elementary or secondary education will find the reasoning we have put forth here to be familiar. What we have described here directly parallels a very similar movement in the field of education. The work of Cronbach and Snow (1977) on aptitude treatment interactions, Hunt's (1971) behavior-person-environment matching model, and Klausmeier, Rossmiller, and Saily's (1977) individually guided education are but three of several examples of prescriptive intervention strategies that have emerged in recent years.

adolescent offenders who are neurotic (Empey, 1969), who display some reasonable level of prosocial behavior (Garrity, 1956) or social maturity (Sealy & Banks, 1971), or who are, in the terminology of the interpersonal (I-level) maturity system, Cultural Conformists (California Department of the Youth Authority, 1967). Probation may well be a considerably less than optimal prescription when the youth is nonneurotic (Empey, 1969), manipulative (Garrity, 1956), or low in social maturity (Sealy & Banks, 1971).

Individual Psychotherapy

Individual psychotherapy has been shown to be effective with highly anxious adolescents (Adams, 1962), the socially withdrawn (Stein & Bogin, 1978), those displaying at most a moderate level of psychopathic behavior (Carney, 1966; Craft, Stephenson, & Granger, 1964), and youngsters who display a set of characteristics summarized by Adams (1961) as "amenable." Youngsters who are more blatantly psychopathic, who manifest a low level of anxiety, or those who are "nonamenable" in Adams's (1961) terms are appropriately viewed as poor candidates for individual psychotherapy interventions. Thus, once again, depending on the type of youngster involved, a given treatment may or may not be appropriate.

Group Psychotherapy

Many group approaches have been developed in attempts to aid aggressive, withdrawn, or immature adolescents. Some of the more popular have been activity group therapy (Slavson, 1964), guided group interaction (McCorkle, Elias, & Bixby, 1958), and positive peer culture (Vorrath & Brendtro, 1974). Research demonstrates that such approaches are indeed useful for older, more sociable and person-oriented adolescents (Knight, 1969), for those who tend to be confrontation-accepting (Warren, 1974), and for the more neurotic-conflicted (Harrison & Mueller, 1964) and the acting-out neurotic (California Department of the Youth Authority, 1967). Youngsters who are younger, less sociable, or more delinquent (Knight, 1969), or who are confrontation-avoiding (Warren, 1974) or psychopathic (Craft et al., 1964), are less likely to benefit from group intervention.

Behavior Modification

In recent years, a host of therapeutic procedures have been developed and proffered under the rubric of behavior modification. While withdrawn (O'Connor, 1972) and immature youngsters have been the recipients of some useful behavioral treatments, most of the focus has centered upon the aggressive, oppositional, or delinquent adolescent (Bernal, Duryee, Pruett, & Burns, 1968; Braukmann & Fixsen, 1976; Drabman, Spitalnik, & O'Leary, 1973; Patterson & Reid, 1973; Stumphauser, 1972; Wahler, 1969). As Braukmann and Fixsen (1976) note, the more effective behavior modification programs typically include (1) a teaching component (e.g., modeling, shaping) designed to add the desired behavior to the adolescent's repertoire, (2) an incentive component (e.g., token economy, behavioral contract) to motivate the youngster, and (3) the actual delivery of reinforcement contingent upon performance of the desired behavior. Literally dozens of specific techniques incorporating one or more of these components have been developed. As Turkat and Feuerstein (1978) observe, even though behavior modification has been the focus of much more experimental scrutiny than any other orientation, a great deal of evaluative research still must be done before the effectiveness of such interventions is firmly established. We would add to their admonition by proposing that the outcomes of such research are much more likely to be positive if the treatments thus considered are planned, implemented, and evaluated prescriptively.

SUMMARY

This brief prescriptive view of the array of interventions currently in use for adolescents—incarceration, probation, individual and group psychotherapy, other group approaches, and a number of behavior modification efforts—shows that they all converge on the same conclusion. We disagree with Bailey (1966), Martinson (1974), Vinter and Janowitz (1959), Kassenbaum, Ward, & Wilner (1972), and others who have concluded that no treatment approach is effective in remediating the behavioral problems of adolescents, i.e., that "nothing works." In considering relevant research literature, they have succumbed to the influence of the one true light assumption. It is not correct that "nothing works." On the contrary, almost everything works—but only for certain youngsters. To be sure, our prescriptive sophistication for the treatment of adolescents is at a mere beginning. The relatively few adolescent characteristics that can be defined as amenable to each treatment considered above clearly show the rudimentary level of prescriptive matching now possible. But it is indeed a beginning. The task, therefore, is to develop and continuously refine an array of treatment and training programs and to engage in research that enables us to make even better matches of practitioners, youngsters, and treatment approaches. How such research is optimally planned, executed, and evaluated has been considered elsewhere (Goldstein, 1978; Goldstein & Stein, 1976).

The remainder of this book is devoted to a presentation of one prescriptive approach, Structured Learning. It is a psychoeducational intervention designed specifically to enhance the prosocial, interpersonal, stress management, and planning skills of the aggressive, withdrawn, immature, and "normal" but developmentally lagging adolescent. It is prescriptively appropriate to the degree that the youngster is behaviorally deficient in such skills. Chapter 2 describes the development of Structured Learning, and Chapter 3 describes its procedures in considerable detail. Chapter 4 will explore how and when Structured Learning is prescriptively appropriate. Chapter 5 will provide the reader with the skill materials necessary to actually conduct Structured Learning sessions. The details of an initial session (Chapter 6) and the management of various problems and resistances that may arise during Structured Learning sessions (Chapter 7) are also presented. Chapter 8 presents the results of a prescriptive research program evaluating the effectiveness of Structured Learning, seeking thereby to point to further research directions of potential yield for the treatment of adolescents.

CHAPTER 2

Structured Learning: Background and Development

A new helping movement, the psychoeducational training movement, is growing in the United States. Its chief characteristic is the combined use of various didactic, instructional, and audiovisual techniques to train individuals in the interpersonal, prosocial, cognitive, or other personal skills in which they may be deficient. Consistent with educational thinking and terminology, the broad goal of psychoeducational training is skill competence and its chief consequent: effective and satisfying daily living. Thus, in the typical psychoeducational training session, skill-deficient trainees are shown examples of competent skill behavior, given opportunities to rehearse what they have seen, provided with systematic feedback regarding the adequacy of their performance, and encouraged in a variety of ways to use their new skills in their real-life environment. This chapter and the one that follows will show in detail the learning procedures that constitute such a training approach. First, however, the historical antecedents of the psychoeducational training movement will be examined.

PSYCHOLOGICAL ANTECEDENTS

While psychoeducational training, as a term and as a reality, may be said to have begun in the early 1970s, its roots are long and diverse. One must point first to the fact that the primary concern of psychology, since its formal inception in America, has been to understand and enhance the learning process. Clinical application of research into the learning process started in the 1950s, as therapists and theoreticians alike came more and more to view treatment in learning terms. Clients or patients needed to learn more adaptive methods with which to cope with the variety of problems for which they sought help. The very healthy and still-expanding field of behavior modification grew from this joint learning-clinical focus and may be viewed as the context in which psychoeducational training efforts were first developed. In most behavioral approaches, as is true of psychoeducational training, specific target behaviors are selected as the goals for remediation or enhancement, laboratory-derived learning procedures are implemented toward these goals, the change agent functions as teacher-trainer, and the success or failure of the effort is judged in terms of observable, behavioral criteria.

In the 1960s, American psychiatry and psychology more and more proclaimed that remediation was not enough. In this, the community mental health era, *prevention* became the byword. This view held that practitioners should not wait until inadequacies were demonstrated before trying to undo them. Rather, it was held, individuals should be trained *in advance* to meet life's challenges, hopefully necessitating less need for remedial action at later points. Quite clearly, psychoeducational skill training was a direct expression of such preventive thinking.

EDUCATIONAL ANTECEDENTS

In addition to the growing importance of learning methods in applied clinical work and the preventive focus in community mental health, there were parallel developments in education that clearly encouraged psychoeducational training. Growing from the personal-development context fostered by such earlier educational movements as progressive education (Dewey, 1938) and character education (Chapman, 1977), a number of other educational approaches have been developed. Their goals are not enhancement of academic skills but, instead, the teaching of concepts and behaviors relevant to values, morality, and emotional functioning. We refer in particular to values clarification (Simon, Howe, & Kirschenbaum, 1972), moral education (Kohlberg, 1973), and affective education (Miller, 1976). These three approaches, as well as such other personal growth programs in educational contexts as identity education (Weinstein & Fantini, 1970), psychosocial training (Ryan & Hoffman, 1973), sensitivity consideration groups (McPhail, Ungold-

Thomas, & Chapman, 1975), human relations training (Bradford, Gibb, & Benne, 1964), confluent education (Castillo, 1974), and psychosynthesis (Assagioli, 1965), all combine to provide a supportive climate and context for psychoeducational training. All of these programs share a concern for personal development, competence, and social effectiveness. Education, in a formal classroom sense, has clearly been broadened well beyond basic academic content into areas that have traditionally been the concern of mental health practitioners.

To be sure, not everyone shares this expanded view of what might constitute this broadened educational philosophy or curriculum. As Authier, Gustafson, Guerney, and Kasdorf (1975) observe, there are many who prefer formal education to consist of the three R's and similar subjects, leaving such concerns as morality, character development, social competence, coping skills, and other domains of psychological education to either "natural" development (i.e., nonintervention) or to parents and/or church. However, viewed over a long time span, psychological education has certainly become a legitimate part of today's educational curriculum.

COMPONENTS OF STRUCTURED LEARNING

We wish to turn at this point to the major focus of this book, the psychoeducational training approach we have termed Structured Learning, and examine its four components in detail. Structured Learning consists of (1) modeling, (2) role playing, (3) performance feedback, and (4) transfer of training. The trainee is shown numerous specific and detailed examples (either live or on audiotape, videotape, film, or filmstrip) of a person (the model) performing the skill behaviors we wish the trainee to learn (i.e., modeling). The trainee is given considerable opportunity and encouragement to rehearse or practice the behaviors that have been modeled (i.e., role playing) and provided with positive feedback, approval, or praise as the role playing of the behaviors becomes more and more similar to the behavior of the model (i.e., performance feedback). Finally, the trainee is exposed to procedures which are designed to increase the likelihood that the newly learned behaviors will in fact actually be applied in a stable manner in class, at home, at work, or elsewhere (i.e., transfer of training).

Modeling

Modeling is defined as learning by imitation. Imitation has been examined in a great deal of research and under many names: copying, empathic learning, observational learning, identification, vicarious learning, matched-dependent behavior, and, most frequently, modeling. This research has consistently shown that modeling is an effective and reliable technique for both the rapid learning of new behaviors and the strengthening or weakening of previously learned behaviors. Three types of learning by modeling have been identified.

1. *Observational learning* refers to the learning of *new* behaviors that the person has never performed before. Adolescents are great imitators. Almost weekly, new idioms, new clothing styles, new ways of talking, walking, dancing, and doing emerge and, with fad-like swiftness, seem to take hold in the world of adolescence. Many of these events are clear examples of observational learning effects.

2. *Inhibitory and disinhibitory effects* involve the strengthening or weakening of behaviors previously performed only rarely by the person due to a history of punishment or other negative reactions. Modeling offered by peers is, again, a major source of inhibitory and disinhibitory effects. Youngsters who know how to be altruistic, sharing, caring, and the like may inhibit such behaviors in the presence of models who are behaving more egocentrically and being rewarded for their egocentric behavior. Aggressive models may also have a disinhibitory effect and cause the observing youngster to engage in aggressive behavior. Later in this book, when such skills as "Dealing with Group Pressure" are discussed, ways of teaching youngsters how to avoid such disinhibitory effects will be explored.

3. *Behavioral facilitation* refers to the performance of previously learned behaviors that are neither new nor a source of potential negative reactions from others. One person buys something he seems to enjoy, so a friend buys one, too. A child deals with a recurring household matter in an effective manner, so a sibling imitates her behavior. A classmate tries talking over a class problem with her teacher; when she succeeds, a second student decides to approach the teacher in a similar way. These are all examples of behavioral facilitation effects.

Research has demonstrated that a wide variety of behaviors can be learned, strengthened, weakened, or facilitated through modeling.

These include acting aggressively, helping others, behaving independently, planning careers, becoming emotionally aroused, interacting socially, displaying dependency, exhibiting certain speech patterns, behaving empathically, self-disclosing, and many more. It is clear from such research that modeling can be an important tool in teaching new behaviors.

Yet it is also true that most people observe dozens and perhaps hundreds of behaviors every day that they do not imitate. Many people are exposed (by television, radio, magazines, and newspapers) to very polished, professional modeling displays of someone buying one product or another, but they do not later buy the product. And many people observe expensively produced and expertly acted instructional films, but they remain uninstructed. Apparently, people learn by modeling under some circumstances but not others. Laboratory research on modeling has successfully identified what we have called ''modeling enhancers,'' a number of circumstances that increase modeling. These modeling enhancers are characteristics of the model, the modeling display, or the trainee (the observer) that have been shown to significantly affect the degree to which learning by imitation occurs.

Modeling Enhancers

Model Characteristics.   More effective modeling will occur when the model (the person to be imitated) (a) seems to be highly skilled or expert; (b) is of high status; (c) controls rewards desired by the trainee; (d) is of the same sex, approximate age, and social status as the trainee; (e) is friendly and helpful; and, of particular importance, (f) is rewarded for the given behaviors. That is, we are all more likely to imitate expert or powerful yet pleasant people who receive rewards for what they are doing, especially when the particular rewards involved are something that we, too, desire.

Modeling Display Characteristics.   More effective modeling will occur when the modeling display shows the behaviors to be imitated (a) in a clear and detailed manner; (b) in the order from least to most difficult behaviors; (c) with enough repetition to make overlearning likely; (d) with as little irrelevant (not to be learned) detail as possible; and (e) when several different models, rather than a single model, are used.

Observer (Trainee) Characteristics. More effective modeling will occur when the person observing the model is (a) told to imitate the model; (b) similar to the model in background or in attitude toward the skill; (c) friendly toward or likes the model; and, most important, (d) rewarded for performing the modeled behaviors.

The effects of these modeling enhancers, as well as of modeling itself, can be better understood by examination of the three stages of learning by modeling.

Stages of Modeling

Attention. Trainees cannot learn from watching a model unless they pay attention to the modeling display and, in particular, to the specific behaviors being modeled. Such attention is maximized by eliminating irrelevant detail in the modeling display, minimizing the complexity of the modeled material, making the display vivid, and implementing the modeling enhancers previously described.

Retention. In order to later reproduce the behaviors he has observed, the trainee must remember or retain them. Since the behaviors of the modeling display itself are no longer present, retention must occur by memory. Memory is aided if the behaviors displayed are classified or coded by the observer. Another name for such coding is "covert rehearsal," i.e., reviewing in one's mind the performance of the displayed behaviors. Research has shown, however, that an even more important aid to retention is overt, or behavioral, rehearsal. Such practice of the specific behavioral steps is crucial for learning and, indeed, is the second major procedure of Structured Learning. This is role playing, a procedure that will be examined in depth shortly. It should be noted at this point, however, that the likelihood of retention via either covert or overt rehearsal is greatly aided by rewards being provided to both the model and/or the trainee.

Reproduction. Researchers interested in human learning have typically distinguished between learning (acquiring or gaining knowledge about how to do something) and performance (doing it). If a person has paid attention to and remembered the behaviors shown on the modeling display, it may be said that the person has learned. The main interest, however, is not so much in whether the person *can* reproduce the behaviors that have been seen, but whether he *does* reproduce them. As with retention, the likelihood that a person will actually perform the behavior that has been learned will depend mostly on the expectation of a reward for doing so. Expectation of reward has been shown to be determined by the amount, consistency, recency, and frequency of the reward that the trainee has observed being provided to the model for performing the desired behaviors. The crucial nature of reward for performance shall be further examined later in this chapter.

Research on Modeling

A great deal of research has been done on the effectiveness of modeling in real-life settings. Lefkowitz, Blake, and Mouton (1954), for example, examined the effect of a model on the frequency of pedestrian traffic violations. These researchers arranged to have an individual (the model) either cross a street or wait to cross during a period in which a ''wait'' pedestrian traffic signal was lit. The imitative behavior (crossing or waiting) of over 2,000 pedestrians was observed. The results indicated that significantly* more pedestrians crossed against the ''wait'' signal when the model crossed than when the model waited or when no model was present.

Research reported by Bryan and Test (1967) shows that helpful behavior can also be modeled. In their first research report, entitled ''Lady in Distress,'' an automobile with a flat left-rear tire was parked on a busy Los Angeles street. A young woman was stationed by the car, and an inflated tire was leaned against the left side of the car. The car, the girl, the flat tire, and the spare were in clear view of the passing traffic. For four of the eight hours that the experiment lasted, a second auto was parked on the same street one-quarter mile before the car described above. This car was raised by a jack under its left rear bumper, and a young woman was watching a man (the model) changing a flat tire. This was the study's modeling procedure. The rest of the time, no such model was present. During the study, 4,000 vehicles passed the two cars. Significantly more drivers stopped at the second car and offered to help the stranded motorist when the model was present than when the model was not present.

---

*Significantly (or ''statistically significant'') will be used throughout this book in the technical sense, i.e., such a result is very likely a ''real'' result, one that occurs by chance less than five times in a hundred.

A second, similar study was conducted by the same researchers at a Princeton, New Jersey, shopping center. Here the procedure involved a model going up to a Salvation Army kettle, placing a donation in it, and walking away. Again, a modeling effect was shown. Significantly more passersby made a donation when the model had just done so.

Bandura (1973) views the acquisition of aggressive behaviors in youngsters as learned initially through the effects of modeling. In a large number of studies, Bandura and his colleagues demonstrated that youngsters do in fact exhibit more aggressive behaviors when vivid modeling displays of such behaviors are presented to them. In one of these original studies, Bandura, Ross, and Ross (1961) showed that children who observed models behave in physically and verbally aggressive ways toward a large plastic figure subsequently acted in similarly aggressive ways in a variety of situations to a significantly greater degree than did children not exposed to such aggressive models. Such observational learning of aggression by youngsters is a frequently replicated research finding (e.g., Fairchild & Erwin, 1977; Kirkland & Thelen, 1977; Rosenthal, 1976).

Evidence is also impressive in demonstrating the effectiveness of modeling as a technique for teaching a variety of behaviors in other diverse situations. For example, modeling has been used to enhance self-disclosure of personal concerns in interview situations (Marlatt, Jacobson, Johnson, & Morrice, 1970), to increase the interviewee's liking for the interviewers (Friedenberg, 1971; Walsh, 1971), to decrease anxiety about public speaking (Kleinsasser, 1968), and to reduce schoolchildren's fears about examinations (Mann, 1972). Indeed, a great deal of learning, both in everyday situations and in laboratory or clinical settings, can be attributed to the effects of modeling. Furthermore, modeling is particularly effective with children and adolescents. In addition to dealing with the aggressive behavior noted above, modeling has been used successfully with youngsters to teach social affiliativeness (Evers & Schwarz, 1973), creativity (Zimmerman & Dialissi, 1973), self-control (Toner, Moore, & Ashley, 1978), sharing (Canale, 1977; Grusec, Kuczynski, Rushton, & Simutis, 1978; Rogers-Warren & Baer, 1976), certain cognitive skills (Lowe & Cuvo, 1976), and even imitation itself (Kaufman, Gordon, & Baker, 1978).

Modeling—Necessary But Insufficient

The positive outcome of these modeling studies may raise questions about the need for the other components of Structured Learning. If so many types of behavior have been changed successfully by watching a model, why are role playing, performance feedback, and transfer of training necessary? Our answer is clear: modeling alone is not enough because its many positive effects are very often short-lived. For example, ministers who were taught (by modeling) to be more empathic when conducting interviews were more empathic immediately after training, but a very short time later their increased empathy had disappeared (Perry, 1970). A modeling study of empathy with nurses and hospital aides produced the same result (Sutton, 1970). Earlier it was noted that learning appears to be improved when the learner has the opportunity and is encouraged to practice, rehearse, or role play the behaviors he has seen performed by the model and when he is rewarded for doing so. In other words, viewing the modeling display teaches the trainee *what* to do. In addition, he needs enough practice to learn *how* to do it and sufficient reward to motivate him or, in effect, to answer the question of *why* he should behave in certain ways. Let us now turn to the *how* question —to the second component of Structured Learning, role playing.

Role Playing

Role playing has been defined as ''a situation in which an individual is asked to take a role [behave in certain ways] not normally his own, or if his own, in a place not normal for the enactment of the role'' (Mann, 1956). The use of role playing to help a person change her behavior or attitudes has been a popular approach for many years.

Perhaps as many as a hundred studies have been done, mostly aimed at discovering the effects of role playing on attitude change. In the typical experiment of this type, the research subjects are first given some sort of attitude questionnaire. One of the attitude dimensions on this questionnaire is selected for the study. The subjects are then placed in one of three experimental groups. Those assigned to the role-playing group are requested to make a speech or other public statement in support of attitudes that are *opposite* to those they really believe. That is, they must actively defend a viewpoint that is opposed to theirs. Subjects in the second group, the exposure group, hold the same private attitudes as the role-playing subjects but are not requested to make such a speech opposite to their real attitudes. They simply are required to listen to one of the speeches made by a role-playing subject. Control-group subjects neither make nor hear such a speech. All subjects are then given the attitude questionnaire a second time. This type of experiment has consistently shown that role-playing subjects change in their attitudes (away from what they privately believed toward what they publicly said) significantly more than either exposure or control subjects.

Role-Play Enhancers

Studies such as those previously mentioned form an impressive demonstration of the value of role playing for behavior and attitude change. However, as with modeling, behavior or attitude change through role playing will occur and be lasting only if certain conditions are met. If the role player has enough information about the content of the role to enact it and if sufficient attention has been paid to what may be called role-play enhancers, it is more likely that behavior or attitude change will result. These role-play enhancers include (a) choice on the part of the trainee regarding whether to take part in the role playing; (b) trainee commitment to the behavior or attitude he is role playing in the sense that the enactment of the role is public rather than private, or otherwise difficult to disown; (c) improvisation in enacting the role-play behaviors; and (d) reward, approval, or reinforcement for enacting the role-play behaviors.

Research on Role Playing

One rather dramatic use of role playing is a study conducted by Janis and Mann (1965) aimed at decreasing smoking. Their research subjects were 26 young women who were all smokers. The women were asked to assume a role in which they were medical patients awaiting the results of a series of diagnostic tests they had just undergone. The experimenter took the part of a physician. Half of the women were asked to enact the role of patient (role players), and the other 13 listened to tape recordings of the role players. The role players individually acted five scenes with the physician, all of which were designed to arouse fear. Scene one involved role playing in a waiting room. The role player was encouraged to express fear regarding the outcome of the diagnosis. The second scene involved a conversation with the physician at which time the role player learned that she had lung cancer and that surgery was necessary. During the third scene, she expressed her concern about the diagnosis; during the fourth scene, she discussed the hospital arrangements and the moderate likelihood of a successful outcome. The fifth scene involved a conversation with the physician about the relationship between smoking and lung cancer. Results indicated that the role players' attitudes about the relationship between smoking and lung cancer and their willingness to try to stop smoking changed significantly more often than did the attitudes of those who just listened to tape recordings of the scenes. Furthermore, it is certainly of greater importance from a behavioral viewpoint that the role players were actually smoking significantly fewer cigarettes per day.

A second impressive demonstration of the effects of role playing has been reported by McFall and Marston (1970). They worked with 42 people who felt that they were too unassertive and dependent. The purpose of the role playing was to increase assertive and independent behavior. The researchers developed 24 situations which the subject was asked to listen to and then respond to by role playing what an assertive person might say and do. For example, in one situation the subject heard:

> Narrator: Imagine that this morning you took your car to a local Standard station, and you explicitly told the mechanic to give you a simple tune-up. The bill should have been about $20. It is now later in the afternoon and you're at the station to pick up your car. The mechanic is walking over to you. . . .
>
> Mechanic: Okay, let me make out a ticket for you. The tune-up was $12 for parts and $8 for labor. Uh, grease and oil job was $6. Antifreeze was $5. Uh, $4 for a new oil filter, and, uh, $5 for rotating the tires. That's $40 in all. Will this be cash or charge?

Subjects were encouraged and helped to role play assertive responses to the situations. They were given coaching on their directness, tone of voice, inflection, communication of feeling, and so forth. After completion of these procedures, role players were compared in terms of several measures of assertiveness with other subjects who had discussed, but not role played, being more assertive and still others who had neither role played nor discussed assertiveness. The role players were not only significantly more assertive on these measures, but also were significantly less anxious about being assertive. McFall and Marston then tried to find out if the role-play training had any affect on the assertiveness of subjects in their real-life behavior. Two weeks after their role-play participation, each subject was telephoned by a different experimenter posing as a magazine salesperson. Working from a prepared script, the salesperson delivered a hard-sell pitch for magazine subscriptions. The telephone call was terminated only (1) after the subject agreed to buy, (2) after five minutes had passed without a sale, (3) after all sales gambits had been used without success, or (4) after the subject had hung up on the salesperson. Analysis of these telephone conversations revealed that the subjects who had undergone role playing showed strong sales resistance at a significantly earlier point in the telephone call than did other groups of subjects.

Using the same or very similar experimental procedures, role players have shown significantly more behavior and attitude change than observers or controls on such dimensions as school attendance (Shoabs, 1964), social skills (Hubbel, 1954), acceptance of minority children (Nichols, 1954), interpersonal sensitivity in classroom settings (Chesler & Fox, 1966), attitudes toward another person (Davis & Jones, 1960), moral judgment (Arbuthnot, 1975; Mately & Acksen, 1976), conflict management skills (Spivack & Shure, 1974), altruism (Iannotti, 1977), empathy (Staub, 1971), and a variety of other social skills (Rathjen, Hiniker, & Rathjen, 1976; Ross, Ross, & Evans, 1976). This small sample of research demonstrates that role playing can lead to many types of behavior and attitude change.

Role Playing—Necessary But Insufficient

Thus far, considerable evidence for the value of role-playing procedures in fostering behavior change has been presented. As with modeling, role playing may be seen as a necessary though insufficient behavior change technique. Its effects, as when modeling is used alone, often do not last. Three investigations on the effects of role playing on smoking failed to demonstrate any lasting behavioral change (Lichtenstein, Keutzer, & Himes, 1969). Furthermore, a very careful study reported by Hollander (1970) found no behavior change due to role playing, even though choice, commitment, improvisation, and reward were all reflected in her procedures. Thus, in most attempts to help a person change his behavior, neither modeling alone nor role playing alone is enough. Combining the two is an improvement, for then the trainee knows both what to do and how to do it. But even this combination is insufficient, for the trainee still needs to know why he should behave in new ways. That is, a motivational or incentive component must be added to the "training package." It is for this purpose that performance feedback is now considered.

Performance Feedback

Performance feedback is defined as providing a trainee with information on how well she has done during role playing. It may take such forms as reward, reinforcement, criticism, or reteaching. The present discussion of performance feedback will emphasize social reinforcement, i.e., praise, approval, and encouragement, because such reinforcement has been shown to be an especially potent influence on behavior change. The nature and effects of reinforcement have received more study than any other aspect of the learning process.*

Reinforcement

Reinforcement typically has been defined as any event that serves to increase the likelihood that a given behavior will occur. Three types of reinforcement have been described: (1) material reinforcement, such as food or money; (2) social reinforcement, such as praise or approval from others; and (3) self-reinforcement, which is a person's positive evaluation of his own behavior. Effective training must give proper attention to all three types of reinforcement. Material reinforcement may be viewed as a necessary base, without which the "higher" levels of reinforcement (social and self) may not function. For many trainees, material reinforcement may be the only

---

*The earlier discussion of the reproduction phase of modeling briefly mentioned the difference between learning and performance. Learning refers to acquiring knowledge—coming to know how to do something, the perception and storage of stimulus-response relationships. Learning defined this way is an internal process and, as such, cannot be observed directly. Performance refers to action—doing what was learned. Many researchers take the position that the main effects of reinforcement are on performance, i.e., on the occurrence and nature of how and when what is learned is actually enacted.

class of reinforcement to which they will respond at first. But there is considerable evidence that behavior that has changed in response to a program of only material rewards typically disappears (extinguishes) when the rewards are no longer forthcoming. It is for this reason that an effort is usually made to pair social reinforcers with material reinforcers and, eventually, to eliminate material reinforcers while retaining social rewards. In real-life settings, a job well done receives a verbal "nice job" more often than a tangible reward, and helping a friend with a chore elicits "thanks" or approval, not money or objects. In other words, it is important that a skill-training effort not rely too heavily or too long on material reinforcers. Social reinforcers can and should be used as an important component of effective skill training.

Even though social reinforcers may be more likely and, hence, more valuable than material reinforcers in the real-life sense described above, it is also true that many valuable real-life behaviors go unnoticed, uncommented upon, and unappreciated by others. Therefore social reinforcement, too, may at times be an unreliable ally in the skill-training enterprise. Such potential social reinforcement suppliers as teachers, parents, and friends may often be either nonrewarding or simply unavailable. If, however, trainees can be aided in becoming their own reinforcement suppliers, if they can be helped to evaluate their own skill behaviors and reward or approve their own effective performance, a very major stride will have been made toward increasing the chances that newly learned skills will be performed in a reliable and enduring manner in real-life settings.

Reinforcement Enhancers

Thus far, reinforcement has been defined, the nature and consequences of different types of reinforcement have been indicated, and its importance for human performance has been emphasized. In looking for effective training methods, it is insufficient to simply acknowledge that reinforcement is a crucial ingredient in the training process; the effectiveness and permanence of the effect of feedback (in the form of reinforcement) in determining performance will depend on several characteristics of the reinforcements used. These characteristics, or reinforcement enhancers, are now discussed.

Type of Reinforcement. As McGehee and Thayer (1961) have

observed, ''What one person regards as a rewarding experience may be regarded by another as neutral or nonrewarding, or even punishing'' (p. 140). While it is obviously true that certain types of reinforcers, such as approval, food, affection, and money, have a high likelihood of serving as effective reinforcers for most people most of the time, this will not always be the case. Both the individual's own reinforcement history and his needs at the time will affect whether the intended reinforcer is, in fact, reinforcing. It is desirable, therefore, that all training procedures take account of and respond to the individual reinforcement histories and current needs of the participating trainees. This means choosing not only between given material, social, and self-reinforcers when necessary, but also making changes in these choices in a continuing and sensitive manner.

Delay of Reinforcement. Laboratory research on learning has shown consistently that behavior change occurs most effectively when the reinforcement follows immediately after the desired behavior. Reinforcement strengthens the behavior that was going on just before the reinforcement took place and makes it likely that the behavior will occur again. Thus, it is possible that delayed reinforcement can lead to the strengthening of inappropriate or ineffective behaviors if such behaviors occur between the desired behavior and the onset of reinforcement.

Response-Contingent Reinforcement. Related to the issue of immediate versus delayed reinforcement are other matters of timing that aid or inhibit the effects of reinforcement on performance. Bandura (1969) has commented:

> In many instances considerable rewards are bestowed, but they are not made conditional upon the behavior that change agents wish to promote . . . special privileges, activities, and rewards are generally furnished according to fixed time schedules rather than performance requirements, and, in many cases, positive reinforcers are inadvertently made contingent upon the wrong types of behavior. (pp. 229-230)

Thus, it is clear that the contingent relationship or linkage between performance and reinforcement must be reflected in training procedures and made sufficiently clear to the trainee.

Amount and Quality of Reinforcement. In addition to the considerations noted above—concerning type, timing, and contingency of the reinforcement provided—the amount and quality of reinforcement are major determinants of performance. With certain important exceptions, the greater the amount of reinforcement, the greater the positive effect upon performance. One limitation on this principle is that increases in certain types of reinforcement do increase performance, but in smaller and smaller amounts. Research on the amount of reinforcement serves as further illustration of the difference between learning and performance. In the laboratory at least, subjects do not appear to learn (acquire new knowledge) more rapidly for large rewards than for small ones. Once learning has taken place, however, performance will often be more dependable if larger rewards are provided.

Opportunity for Reinforcement. A further requirement for successful and consistent performance is that the behavior to be reinforced must occur with sufficient frequency that reinforcement can be provided. If such behaviors are too infrequent, insufficient opportunity will exist to influence them through contingent reinforcement. Beyond its several types of practice effects noted earlier, role playing provides excellent opportunities to reinforce behavior.

Partial (Intermittent) Reinforcement. Partial reinforcement refers to the reinforcement of only some of the person's correct responses by reinforcing at fixed times (e.g., at the end of each class), at a fixed number of responses (e.g., every fifth correct response), on a variable time or response schedule (e.g., randomly choosing—within limits—the time or correct response to reward), and on other schedules. In all instances, it has been consistently shown that behaviors that have been intermittently reinforced are longer lasting than behaviors reinforced each time they occur.

In summary of this discussion of reinforcement, research evidence indicates that high levels of performance are likely to occur if the trainees are given sufficient opportunity to receive immediate reinforcements of a kind that is right for them in sufficiently large amounts which are offered in a response-contingent manner on an intermittent schedule.

There is considerable evidence supporting the behavior change impact of modeling, role playing, and reinforcement. We have held that neither modeling alone nor role playing alone yields results nearly as effective as the two combined. We now wish to take a similar position regarding reinforcement. While it is true that reinforcement alone is more likely to lead to lasting behavior change than either modeling or role playing alone, it is also true that the behaviors to be reinforced must occur with sufficient correctness and sufficient frequency for reinforcement to have its intended effect. The addition of modeling insures that the behavior to be reinforced will be the correct behavior. Providing opportunity for role playing or practice of correct behaviors insures that they will occur with sufficient frequency. Yet there is one further component of Structured Learning to consider, a component responsive to the ultimate purpose of any training endeavor: transfer of what has been learned from the training setting to the real-life setting.

Transfer of Training

The main interest of any training program (and where most training programs fail) is not in the trainees' performance in the training site but, instead, in how well they perform in their real lives. If skills have been satisfactorily performed at the time of training, what procedures are available to maximize the chances that such performance will continue in a durable manner on the street, in school, at home, or at other places or times where skill use is appropriate? Stated otherwise, how can transfer of training be encouraged?

Research has identified a number of principles of transfer enhancement, the most potent of which we now wish to examine.* While it may prove difficult to implement all of these principles in any given training program, their combined impact is to greatly increase the likelihood of satisfactory positive transfer. These principles will be described below, and in subsequent chapters their implementation in Structured Learning will be examined.

General Principles

Transfer of training has been increased by giving the trainee general principles that govern satisfactory performance in both the training and real-life settings. In other words, the trainee must be given, in a clear and complete manner, the organizing concepts or principles that explain or account for successful skill selection and implementation in both places.

Response Availability (Overlearning)

It has been well established by research that, in a given context,

---

*Several additional means of potential usefulness for increasing transfer of training are described in detail in Goldstein and Kanfer (1979).

practiced behavior or behavior that has occurred most frequently in the past will be likely to occur in the future when a similar situation arises. This principle of transfer originates from research on over-learning, which demonstrates that the higher the degree of original learning, the greater the probability of later transfer. In addition to increasing the likelihood of positive transfer, overlearning may also decrease the chances that negative transfer will occur. When more than one skill is being taught, negative transfer (interference rather than facilitation) is likely to occur if training on the second skill is begun while the first is still only partially learned. This is less likely when correct skill behavior is practiced enough to insure that over-learning has occurred.

Identical Elements

In the earliest experimental work with transfer of training, it was demonstrated that the greater the number of identical elements or characteristics shared by the training and application settings, the greater the later transfer from training to real-life application. Over the years, this finding has been reaffirmed repeatedly. Ideally, both the interpersonal and physical characteristics of the training and application settings would be highly similar. Thus, if possible, train-ees would be trained along with other youngsters with whom they interact regularly. Also, training would take place to the extent feasible in school or at other real-life settings in which youngsters actually interact rather than at a therapy or training center. In addi-tion, the furnishings, materials, and other physical characteristics of the two settings, as well as the nature and scheduling of reinforce-ments, would also be as similar as possible.

Stimulus Variability

Several investigators have demonstrated that positive transfer is greater when a variety of training stimuli are employed (Callantine & Warren, 1955; Duncan, 1958; Shore & Sechrest, 1961). As will be seen in the next chapter, the broad array of interpersonal stimuli represented by the several models, trainers, and role-playing co-actors utilized in Structured Learning readily provides an example of this principle of transfer enhancement. The diverse styles and be-haviors of these several persons all have the potential of serving in application settings as stimuli or cues for desirable behaviors acquired during Structured Learning sessions.

Real-Life Reinforcement

As noted above, in the discussion of response availability, the training needs of the trainee are all too likely to be forgotten once he ''graduates'' from being a trainee and leaves the training site for his real-life setting. The efforts until ''graduation day'' may have been educationally perfect. By whatever training techniques, the trainee may have been brought to an exceedingly high level of performance excellence. The trainer may also have sought to maximize transfer by providing him with general principles, high levels of response availability, maximum identical elements in the training and application settings, and considerable stimulus variability. And yet, given all of these successful efforts, the training may fail if it is discontinued at this point. Training provides skills, information, knowledge, and the potential for their successful application. It is primarily real-life reinforcement—by teachers, parents, peers, and self—that will decide what happens at the application site and that will determine whether the learning acquired will find *enduring* expression in successful performance. Real-life reinforcement to maximize such transfer must be supplemented by corrective feedback for poor quality performance and must continue in real-life settings for satisfactory performance to endure. Such reinforcement must take into account all the dimensions of reinforcement (scheduling, source, nature, amount, etc.) noted earlier as crucial aspects of the training process.

The importance of continued (if intermittent) reinforcement for lasting behavior change should be stressed. Are the new behaviors ignored? Or, as is perhaps more common, are they reinforced at first and then ignored? Continued (if periodic) reinforcement is clearly a necessary enhancer of enduring transfer of training. This principle is sufficiently important that, when implementing a Structured Learning program for adolescents, a trainer (whenever possible) should attempt to teach the value of and the procedures for providing the trainee with continued real-life reinforcement to teachers, parents, principals, peers, and other real-life figures who can provide rewards. To the extent that these efforts have proven successful, a learning cycle is established whereby the likelihood of continued real-life reinforcement, and thus maximal transfer, is increased.

SUMMARY

Four particularly effective procedures for skill training—modeling, role playing, performance feedback, and transfer of training—have been examined in detail. The nature of each, the techniques that maximize their impact, a sample of the wide variety of learning targets to which each has been successfully applied, and samples of supporting research have been presented. Yet, in discussing each procedure, enthusiasm was lessened by one or more cautionary notes. For example, while modeling does indeed result in the learning of new behaviors, without sufficient practice old behaviors clearly tend to recur. Practice or role playing is also an important aid to new learning, but one must practice correct behaviors, and without prior modeling or similar demonstration, the trainee's performance is improved very little over its initial level. Given both modeling and role playing, the newly learned behaviors have greater likelihood of persisting but will not do so unless the trainee sees his use of these behaviors to be a rewarding experience. Thus, this points up the crucial necessity for reinforcement. Even reinforcement, however, is also frequently not enough for effective human learning. The behaviors to be reinforced must be enacted by the trainee correctly and with sufficient frequency that adequate opportunity for reinforcement occurs. Without such procedures, the new behaviors—even if reinforced—may occur too seldom for stable learning to occur. Thus, procedures such as modeling and role playing can lead to such sufficient frequency of correct enactment. Combining these three procedures yields a much more effective and widely applicable approach to skill training, whether the adolescent learner is aggressive, withdrawn, immature, or essentially normal. Yet a truly effective approach to learning must also demonstrate such learning beyond the training setting and must prove to be powerful, broadly applicable, and reliably enduring in the learner's real-life setting. Thus we turned in our presentation to transfer of training. Five principles were described, as were some examples of their use in Structured Learning. The next chapter will describe and illustrate in specific detail the use of these procedures in Structured Learning groups for adolescents.

CHAPTER 3

Structured Learning Procedures for Adolescents

In the present chapter our goal is to provide the reader with specific and detailed instructions for conducting a Structured Learning group. We will discuss matters of organization, trainer preparation, and, in particular, a step-by-step procedural accounting of the modeling-role play-performance feedback-transfer training sequence. Guidelines for optimal trainer behavior in opening and later Structured Learning sessions are also presented. It is our hope that the concrete "how to" information provided in this chapter is of substantial assistance both to individuals wishing to understand Structured Learning better and to those seeking to conduct effective and efficient Structured Learning groups.

ORGANIZING THE STRUCTURED LEARNING GROUP

Selecting Participants

Each Structured Learning group should consist of trainees who are clearly deficient in whatever skills are going to be taught. If possible, trainees should also be grouped according to the degree of deficiency in the given skill. Specific procedures and instruments to help the trainer select and organize an effective Structured Learning group are presented in detail in Chapter 4. Use of these procedures can help identify trainees who are all deficient in certain common skills.

The optimally sized group for effective Structured Learning consists of five to eight trainees plus two trainers.* Those trainees

---

*Another possibility, discussed on pages 49-50, is to implement Structured Learning in a regular-sized class within a school setting. Structured Learning has been employed successfully within such classes as Health, Social Studies, Home Economics, and/or other areas in which some emphasis is placed upon personal and interpersonal development.

selected need not be from the same class or even the same grade. However, since behavioral rehearsal or role playing in the group is most beneficial when it is as realistic as possible, it is often useful to include trainees whose social worlds (family, school, peer groups) have some important elements of similarity. In this way, when a participant is asked to role play a part, this part can be role played in a reasonably accurate fashion.

There are times when it will not be possible to group trainees according to shared skill deficits. Instead, trainers may want to organize groups according to naturally occurring units, such as school classes, residential cottages, etc. If the decision is made to use naturally occurring units, the group members will probably reflect a somewhat broader range of skill strengths and weaknesses. In this case, trainers should select as starting skills those in which many of the class members show a deficiency. In such a potentially divergent group, it is likely that a few class members will be proficient in the use of whatever skill might be taught on a given day. Youngsters who are more adept at the skill being taught can function in helper roles, such as co-actors or providers of useful feedback.

Number, Length, and Spacing of Sessions

The Structured Learning training program can be broken into segments that match part or all of the semesters of the school or training setting. If possible, training should occur at a rate of at least one and, preferably, two times per week. Spacing is crucial in order to provide ample opportunity for students to try out in real life what they have learned in the training setting.

Typically, each training session should focus on learning one skill only. As such, it should include one sequence of modeling, several role plays, feedback, and assignment of homework. Session length should be determined by a number of factors, such as attention span of trainees, impulsivity, verbal ability, etc. One-hour sessions have often proven optimal in schools and other settings. However, if most trainees in a given group show particularly brief attention spans, the session can be as brief as 20 minutes. In such cases, more frequent sessions are advisable. Sessions longer than an hour are possible with trainees whose capacity for sustained attention is greater. Since Structured Learning is intensive, we recommend that sessions not last beyond one and one-half hours because learning efficiency tends to diminish beyond that length of time.

Trainer Preparation

The role-playing and feedback activities that make up most of each Structured Learning session are a series of ''action-reaction'' sequences in which effective skill behaviors are first rehearsed (role played) and then critiqued (feedback). As such, the trainer must both lead and observe. We have found that one trainer is hard pressed to do both of these tasks well at the same time, and thus we strongly recommend that each session be led by a team of two trainers. One trainer can usually pay special attention to the main actor, especially helping him ''set the stage'' and enact the skill's behavioral steps. While this is occurring, the other trainer can attend to the remainder of the group and help them as they observe and evaluate the unfolding role play. The two trainers can then exchange these responsibilities on the next role play.

Two types of trainer skills appear crucial for successfully conducting a Structured Learning group. The first might best be described as General Trainer Skills, i.e., those skills requisite for success in almost any training or teaching effort. These include:

1. Oral communication and teaching ability
2. Flexibility and capacity for resourcefulness
3. Enthusiasm
4. Ability to work under pressure
5. Interpersonal sensitivity
6. Listening skills
7. Knowledge of human behavior, adolescent development, etc.

The second type of requisite skills is Specific Trainer Skills, i.e., those germane to Structured Learning in particular. These include:

1. Knowledge of Structured Learning—its background, procedures and goals
2. Ability to orient both trainees and supporting staff to Structured Learning
3. Ability to plan and present live modeling displays
4. Ability to initiate and sustain role playing
5. Ability to present material in concrete, behavioral form
6. Ability to deal with classroom problems effectively

7. Accuracy and sensitivity in providing corrective feedback.

In school settings, trainers and co-trainers are often regular class-room teachers, aides, guidance counselors, psychologists, resource or special education teachers, volunteers, or even trainees them-selves. We consider the kinds of characteristics described above more important than the particular job title.

For both trainer selection and development purposes, potential trainers should first take the role of trainees in a series of Structured Learning sessions. These sessions are led by two experienced train-ers. After this experience, beginning trainers can then co-lead a series of sessions with an experienced trainer. In this way, trainers can be given several opportunities to practice what they have seen and also to receive feedback regarding their performance. In effect, we recommend the use of the Structured Learning procedures of modeling, role playing, and feedback as the method of choice for training Structured Learning trainers.

PREMEETING PREPARATION OF TRAINEES

Individual preparation of trainees prior to the first meeting of the Structured Learning class may be helpful. This orientation or struc-turing should be tailored to the individual needs and maturity level of each trainee. It should be designed to provide each group member with heightened motivation to attend and participate in the group as well as accurate expectations of what the activities of the group will be like. Methods of trainee preparation might include:

1. Mentioning what the purposes of the group will be as they re-late to the specific skill deficits of the youngster. For example, the trainer might say, ''Remember when you got into a fight with Billy, and you wound up restricted for a week? Well, in this class you'll be able to learn how to stay out of that kind of trouble so you don't get restricted.''

2. Mentioning briefly and generally what procedures will be used. The trainee must have an accurate picture of what to expect. The trainer might say something like, ''In order to learn to handle (these kinds of) situations better, we're going to see and hear some examples of how different kids do it well, and then actually take turns trying some of these ways right here. Then we'll let you know how you did, and you'll have a chance to practice on your own.''

3. Mentioning the benefits to be gained from participation, stating that the group will help the trainee work on particular relevant issues such as getting along in school, at home, and with peers.

4. Mentioning the tangible or token (e.g., points or credits) rewards that trainees will receive for participation.

5. Using the trainer-trainee relationship to promote cooperation. For example, the trainer might ask the youngster, "Give it a try. I think you'll get something out of it."

6. Presenting the Structured Learning class as a new part of the curriculum in which the trainee is expected to participate. Along with the message of expected participation, trainees should also understand that the group is not compulsory and that confidentiality will be respected. A verbal commitment from the youngster to "give it a try" is useful at this point.

7. Mentioning the particular skills that the youngster is likely to identify as her major felt deficiencies and how progress on overcoming these deficiencies might be made by working on such skills.

THE STRUCTURED LEARNING SESSIONS

The Setting

One major principle for encouraging transfer from the classroom and training room to the real-life setting is the rule of identical elements discussed in Chapter 2. This rule states that the more similar or identical the two settings—i.e., the greater number of physical and interpersonal qualities shared by them—the greater the likelihood of transfer from one setting to the other. We urge that Structured Learning be conducted in the same general setting as the real-life environment of most participating trainees and that the training setting be furnished to resemble as much as possible the likely application settings. In a typical classroom, trainers can increase the degree of similarity between classroom and other real-life settings through the creative use of available furniture and supplies. If a couch is needed for a particular role play, several chairs can be pushed together to simulate the couch. If a television set is an important part of a role play, a box, a chair, or a drawing on the chalkboard can, in imagination, approximate the real object. If actual props are available, for example in the form of an actual TV set, store counter, living room furniture, etc., they should certainly be used in the role-play scenes.

The horseshoe seating arrangement illustrated in Figure 1 is one good example of how furniture might be arranged in the training room. Participating trainees sit at desks or tables so that some writing space is provided. Role playing takes place in the front of the room. Behind and to the side of one of the role players is a chalkboard displaying the behavioral steps that make up the skill being worked with at the time. In this way the role player can glance up at the steps during the role play, and one of the trainers, functioning as a coach or prompter, can point to each step as the role play unfolds.

The Opening Session

The opening session is designed to stimulate the trainees' interest in the group and to give more detailed information than was provided in their individual orientation. The trainers open the session with a brief familiarization period or warmup, with the goal of helping participants become comfortable when interacting with the group leaders and with one another. Content for this initial phase should be interesting and nonthreatening to the trainees. Next, trainers introduce the Structured Learning program by providing trainees with a brief description of what skill training is about. Typically this introduction covers such topics as the importance of interpersonal skills for effective and satisfying living, examples of skills that will be taught, and how these skills can be useful to trainees in their everyday lives. It is often helpful to expand upon the discussion of everyday skill use in order to emphasize the importance of the undertaking and its personal relevance to the participants. The specific training procedures (modeling, role playing, etc.) are then described at a level that the group can easily understand. We recommend that trainers describe procedures briefly, with the expectation that trainees will understand them more fully once they have actually participated in their use.

A detailed description of the procedures that ideally make up this opening session are presented in transcript form in Chapter 6.

Modeling

The modeling displays presented to trainees should depict the be-

Figure 1. A Functional Room Arrangement
for Structured Learning

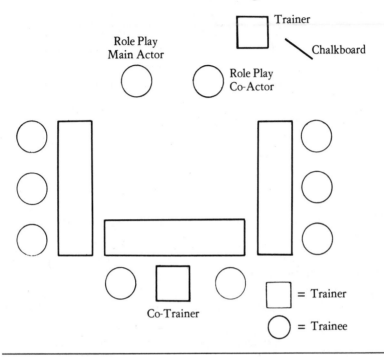

havioral steps that constitute the skill being taught in a clear and unambiguous manner. All of the steps making up the skill should be
modeled, in the correct sequence. Generally, the modeling will consist of live vignettes* enacted by the two trainers, although trainees
may be involved in the modeling displays in some instances. When
two trainers are not available, a reasonably skillful trainee may serve
as a model along with the trainer. In such instances it is especially
important to rehearse the vignettes carefully with the trainee prior
to class, making sure that all of the skill's steps are enacted correctly
and in the proper sequence.

Trainers should plan their modeling displays carefully. Content
should be selected that is relevant to the immediate life situations of
the trainees in the group. At least two examples should be modeled

---

*If available, audio or audiovisual modeling displays, instead of live modeling, may be pre-
sented.

for each skill so that trainees are exposed to skill use in different situations. Thus, two or more different content areas are depicted. We have found that trainers usually do not have to write out scripts for the modeling displays but, instead, plan their roles and likely responses in outline form and rehearse them in their preclass preparations. These modeling display outlines should incorporate the guidelines presented below. For example, the trainers who plan to model the skill of ''Starting a Conversation'' might engage in the following planning:

> Trainer 1: Let's have the first example take place in the principal's office. I'll be the secretary, sitting at the desk. You can be a youngster who wants to start a conversation with me about making an appointment to see the principal. Why don't you walk in and then go through step one by saying. . . .

The guidelines to be kept in mind in developing live modeling displays are:

1. Use at least two examples for each demonstration of a skill. If a skill is used in more than one class meeting, develop two more new modeling displays.

2. Select situations that are relevant to the trainee's real-life circumstances.

3. The main actor, i.e., the person enacting the behavioral steps of the skill, should be portrayed as a youngster reasonably similar in age, socioeconomic background, verbal ability, and other salient characteristics to the youngsters in the Structured Learning group.

4. All displays should depict positive outcomes. There should always be reinforcement to the model who is using the skill well.

5. All modeling displays should depict all the behavioral steps of the skill being modeled, in the correct sequence.

6. Modeling displays should depict only one skill at a time. All extraneous content should be eliminated.

In order to help trainees attend to the skill enactments, Skill Cards, which contain the name of the skill being taught and its behavioral steps, are distributed prior to the modeling displays. Trainees are told to watch and listen closely as the models portray the skill. Particular care should be given to helping trainees identify the behavioral steps as they are presented in the context of the modeling vignettes. Trainers should also remind the youngsters that in order to depict some of the behavioral steps in certain skills, the actors occasionally would be "thinking out loud" statements that would ordinarily be "thought silently" and that this process is done to facilitate learning.

Role Playing

Following the modeling display, discussion should focus on relating the modeled skill to the lives of trainees. Trainers should invite comments on the behavioral steps and how these steps might be useful in real-life situations that trainees encounter. It is most helpful to focus on current and future skill use rather than on only past events or general issues involving the skill. Role playing in Structured Learning is intended to serve as behavioral rehearsal or practice for *future* use of the skill. As such, trainers should be aware that role playing of past events that have little relevance for future situations is of limited value to trainees. However, discussion of past events involving skill use can be relevant in stimulating trainees to think of times when a similar situation might occur in the future. In such a case, the hypothetical future situation rather than a reenactment of the past event would be selected for role playing.

Once a trainee has described a situation in her own life in which skill usage might be helpful, that trainee is designated the main actor. She chooses a second trainee (the co-actor) to play the role of the significant other person (e.g., mother, peer, etc.) in her life who is relevant to the skill problem. The trainee should be urged to pick as a co-actor someone who resembles the real-life person in as many ways as possible. The trainer then elicits from the main actor any additional information needed to set the stage for role playing. In order to make role playing as realistic as possible, the trainers should obtain a description of the physical setting, a description of the events immediately preceding the role play, a description of the co-actor's mood or manner, and any other realism-increasing information of apparent value.

It is crucial that the main actor seek to enact the behavioral steps that have been modeled. *This is the main purpose of the role playing.* Before beginning the actual role playing, the trainer should go over each step as it applies to the role-play situation, thus aiding the main actor in making a successful effort. The main actor is told to refer to the Skill Card on which the behavioral steps are printed. As noted previously, the behavioral steps are written on a chalkboard visible to the main actor as well as the rest of the group during the role playing. Before the role playing begins, trainers should remind all of the participants of their roles and responsibilities: the main actor is told to follow the behavioral steps; the co-actor, to stay in the role of the other person; and the observers, to watch carefully for the enactment of the behavioral steps. For the first several role plays the observers can be coached as to what kinds of cues to observe, e.g., posture, tone of voice, content of speech, etc. Then, the role players are instructed to begin. At this point it is the main responsibility of the trainer to provide the main actor with whatever help or coaching she needs in order to keep the role playing going according to the behavioral steps. Trainees who ''break role'' and begin to explain their behavior or make comments should be urged to get back into the role and explain later. If the role play is clearly going astray from the behavioral steps, the scene can be stopped, needed instruction can be provided, and then the role play can be restarted. One trainer should be positioned near the chalkboard and point to each of the behavioral steps, in turn, as the role play unfolds, thus helping the main actor (as well as the other trainees) to follow each of the steps in order.

The role playing should be continued until all trainees have had an opportunity to participate in the role of main actor. Sometimes this will require two or three sessions for a given skill. We suggest that each session begin with two modeling vignettes for the chosen skill, even if the skill is not new to the group. It is important to note that while the framework (behavioral steps) of each role play in the series remains the same, the actual content can and should change from role play to role play. It is the problem as it actually occurs, or could occur, in each youngster's real-life environment that should be the content of the given role play. When completed, each trainee will thus be better armed to act appropriately in a real situation requiring skill use in his own life.

There are a few further procedural matters relevant to role playing that will serve to increase its effectiveness. Role reversal is often a useful role-play procedure. A trainee role playing a skill may on occasion have a difficult time perceiving his co-actor's viewpoint and vice versa. Having them exchange roles and resume the role play can be most helpful in this regard.

On occasion the trainer can also assume the co-actor role in an effort to give youngsters the opportunity to handle types of reactions not otherwise role played during the session. For example, it may be crucial to have a difficult adult co-actor role realistically portrayed. The trainer as co-actor may also be particularly helpful when dealing with less verbal or more hesitant trainees.

Feedback

A brief feedback period follows each role play. This helps the main actor find out how well he followed or departed from the behavioral steps, examines the psychological impact of the enactment on the co-actor, and provides the main actor with encouragement to try out the role-played behaviors in real life. To implement this process, the trainer should ask the main actor to wait until he has heard everyone's comments before responding to them.

The co-actor is asked about her reactions first. Next the observers comment on how well the behavioral steps were followed and other relevant aspects of the role play. Then the trainers comment in particular on how well the behavioral steps were followed and provide social reinforcement (praise, approval, encouragement) for close following. To be most effective with the use of reinforcement, trainers should follow these guidelines:

1. Provide reinforcement only after role plays that follow the behavioral steps.

2. Provide reinforcement at the earliest appropriate opportunity after role plays that follow the behavioral steps.

3. Always provide reinforcement to the co-actor for being helpful, cooperative, etc.

4. Vary the specific content of the reinforcements offered, e.g., praise particular aspects of the performance, such as tone of voice, posture, phrasing, etc.

5. Provide enough role-playing activity for each group member to have sufficient opportunity to be reinforced.

6. Provide reinforcement in an amount consistent with the quality of the given role play.

7. Provide no reinforcement when the role play departs signifi-

cantly from the behavioral steps (except for ''trying'' in the first session or two).

8. Provide reinforcement for an individual trainee's improvement over previous performances.

After hearing all the feedback, the main actor is invited to make comments regarding the role play and the comments of others. In this way he can learn to evaluate the effectiveness of his skill enactment in the light of evidence from others.

In all aspects of feedback, it is crucial that the trainer maintain the behavioral focus of Structured Learning. Trainer comments must point to the presence or absence of specific, concrete behaviors and not take the form of general evaluative comments or broad generalities. Feedback, of course, may be positive or negative in content. Negative comments should always be followed by a constructive comment as to how a particular fault might be improved. At minimum, a ''poor'' performance (major departures from the behavioral steps) can be praised as ''a good try'' at the same time that it is being criticized for its real faults. If at all possible, youngsters failing to follow the relevant behavioral steps in their role play should be given the opportunity to re-role play these same behavioral steps after receiving corrective feedback. At times, as a further feedback procedure, we have audiotaped or videotaped entire role plays. Giving trainees opportunities to observe themselves on tape can be an effective aid, enabling them to reflect on their own behavior.

Since a primary goal of Structured Learning is skill flexibility, role-play enactment that departs somewhat from the behavioral steps may not be ''wrong.'' That is, a different approach to the skill may in fact ''work'' in some situations. Trainers should stress that they are trying to teach effective alternatives and that the trainees would do well to have the behavioral steps being taught in their repertoire of skill behaviors, available to use when appropriate.

Transfer of Training

Several aspects of the training sessions we have described above are designed to increase the likelihood that learning in the training setting will transfer to the youngster's actual real-life environment. We suggest, however, that even more forthright steps need to be taken to maximize transfer.

Homework Assignments

When possible, we urge use of a homework technique we have found to be successful with most groups. In this procedure trainees are openly instructed to try in their own real-life settings the behaviors they have practiced during the session. The name of the person(s) with whom they will try it, the day, the place, etc., are all discussed. The trainee is urged to take notes on his first transfer attempt on the Homework Report 1 form (see Figure 2) provided by the trainers. This form requests detailed information about what happened when the trainee attempted the homework assignment, how well he followed the relevant behavioral steps, the trainee's evaluation of his performance, and thoughts about what the next assignment might appropriately be.

It has often proven useful to start with relatively simple homework behaviors and, as mastery is achieved, work up to more complex and demanding assignments. This provides the trainer with an opportunity to reinforce each approximation of the more complex target behavior. Successful experiences at beginning homework attempts are crucial in encouraging the trainee to make further attempts at real-life skill use.

The first part of each Structured Learning session is devoted to presenting and discussing these homework reports. When trainees have made an effort to complete their homework assignments, trainers should provide social reinforcement, while failure to do homework should be met with some chagrin and expressed disappointment. It cannot be stressed too strongly that without these or similar attempts to maximize transfer, the value of the entire training effort is in severe jeopardy.

External Support and Self-Reward

Of the several principles of transfer training for which research evidence exists, maximizing real-life reinforcement of skilled behavior is clearly most consequential. Trainees will perform as trained if there is some ''payoff'' for doing so. As we have discussed earlier, new behaviors persist if they are rewarded but diminish if they are ignored or actively challenged.

We have found it useful to implement several supplemental programs outside of the Structured Learning training setting that can

Figure 2. Homework Report 1

Name _____Date_____

Group Leaders_____

FILL IN DURING THIS CLASS

1. What skill will you use?

2. What are the steps for the skill?

3. Where will you try the skill?

4. With whom will you try the skill?

5. When will you try the skill?

FILL IN AFTER DOING YOUR HOMEWORK

1. What happened when you did the homework?

2. Which steps did you really follow?

3. How good a job did you do in using the skill? (Circle one.)

   Excellent   Good   Fair   Poor

4. What do you think should be your next homework assignment?

help to provide the rewards or reinforcements that trainees need in order to maintain their new behaviors. These programs include providing for both external social reward (provided by people in the trainee's real-life environment) and self-reward (provided by the trainee herself).

In several settings, we have actively sought to identify and develop environmental or external support by holding orientation meetings for school staff and for relatives and friends of youngsters, i.e., the real-life reward and punishment givers. These meetings acquaint significant others in the youngster's life with Structured Learning, the skills being taught, and the steps that make up these skills. The most important segment of these sessions involves presenting the procedures whereby staff, relatives, and friends can encourage and reward trainees as they practice their new skills and, thus, help in the transfer effort. We consider these orientation sessions for such persons to be of major value for transfer of training.

Frequently, environmental support is insufficient to maintain newly learned skills. In fact, many real-life environments in which youngsters work and live actually actively resist a youngster's efforts at behavior change. It is not uncommon, for example, for skill-deficient youngsters to have peers who consistently reward antisocial, but not prosocial, behavior. For this reason, we have found it useful to include in our transfer efforts the teaching of self-reinforcement procedures.

After a new skill has been practiced through role playing in the Structured Learning session and the trainee has made his first homework effort and received group feedback, we recommend that trainees continue to practice their new skill as frequently as possible in real-life settings. It is at this time that a program of self-reinforcement can and should be initiated. Trainees can be instructed in the nature of self-reinforcement and encouraged to ''say something and do something nice for yourself'' if they practice their new skill well. Homework Report 2 (see Figure 3) will aid both trainers and trainees in this effort. On this form, trainees can specify potential rewards and indicate how they rewarded themselves for a job well done. The trainee is thus taught to evaluate his own performance even if such efforts do not meet with the hoped-for response from others. For example, if the youngster follows all of the steps of a particular skill

Figure 3. Homework Report 2 (Advanced)

Name _____Date_____

Group Leader _____

FILL IN BEFORE DOING YOUR HOMEWORK

1. What skill will you use?

2. What are the steps for the skill?

3. Where will you try the skill?

4. With whom will you try the skill?

5. When will you try the skill?

6. If you do an excellent job, how will you reward yourself? (What will you say to yourself, and what will you do for yourself?)

7. If you do a good job, how will you reward yourself? (What will you say to yourself, and what will you do for yourself?)

8. If you do a fair job, how will you reward yourself? (What will you say to yourself, and what will you do for yourself?)

FILL IN AFTER DOING YOUR HOMEWORK

1. What happened when you did the homework?

2. Which steps did you really follow?

3. How good a job did you do in using the skill? (Circle one.)

Excellent   Good   Fair   Poor

4. How did you reward yourself?

5. What do you think should be your next homework assignment?

---

well, self-reward might appropriately take the form of saying something (e.g., "I really did that well. I'm proud of myself") and doing something (e.g., "I'll play basketball after school") as a special reward. It is important that these self-rewards are indeed special, i.e., not things that are said or done routinely, but things that are done to acknowledge and reinforce special efforts. Trainees' homework notes can be collected by the trainer in order to keep abreast of independent progress made by trainees without consuming group time. Trainers are cautioned to advance a trainee to this level of independent practice only when he can successfully do what is being asked.

STRUCTURED LEARNING IN A LARGER GROUP

Often it is necessary and/or desirable to employ Structured Learning in a regular-sized class within a school curriculum. Structured Learning may be integrated readily into subject areas that deal with personal or interpersonal development. The interpersonal aspects of such subjects as drugs, alcohol, sex, appearance, family, and peer influences are natural content areas for Structured Learning. However, the size of the group in a regular class is much larger than described in previous sections and requires some modifications of Structured Learning techniques.

While it is possible to conduct modeling displays in a full class of 20 or more trainees, it is desirable to conduct role-playing in smaller groupings. If two trainers are available, this may be done by dividing the large group into two smaller groups for the role playing, with one trainer leading each role-play group. If another trainer is not available, it is certainly possible to utilize a teacher aide, student teacher, parent aide, or other adult who has been oriented to the

Structured Learning procedures. Thus, the whole class would meet as a unit for the discussion of the skill and its modeling and then break into two smaller groups for role playing, feedback, and assignment of homework.

If it is not possible to divide the larger group into two smaller groups, one trainer can conduct Structured Learning with the entire class. In any large group it is expected that a range of skill proficiencies or deficiencies will be evidenced among the trainees. The trainer must make an effort to assess each trainee's relative strengths or weaknesses on the various skills prior to the outset of the Structured Learning sessions. This is done by completing a Skill Checklist for each class member and then transposing their scores to a Grouping Chart. By referring to this chart, the trainer can identify which trainees are deficient in the particular skill being taught. The trainer can thus select as main actors (and co-actors) those trainees who need help in learning the skill.*

In working with a large group whose members are not preselected according to shared skill deficiencies, it is possible to take advantage of the range of trainees' skill proficiencies while still engaging in effective skill building. Specifically, it is often helpful to have trainees who are proficient in a particular skill lead off the role playing in order to set a positive example for less skillful trainees. Skill-proficient trainees can also be incorporated as supportive co-actors in a group with less proficient trainees.

When using Structured Learning with a large class, it is important that the trainer capture the active attention and involvement of as many class members as possible. This can be done by:

1. Using several trainees as co-actors in the role play.

2. Assigning classroom helper roles, e.g., one trainee at the blackboard, one trainee as trainer's helper, etc.

3. Assigning specific observer tasks to all trainees not participating actively in the role play.

It is also possible to divide the large group into smaller discussion groups for part of each class session. In these smaller groups trainees can suggest possible role-play situations for the skill being covered and/or possible homework applications for out-of-class skill use.

---

*The nature and use of the Skill Checklist and the Grouping Chart for optimal selection and grouping are described in detail in Chapter 5.

OUTLINES OF TRAINER PROCEDURES

The material presented in this chapter provides most of what the typical Structured Learning trainer will need to know in order to lead skill-enhancing Structured Learning groups. To assist further, we have provided outlines of procedures that constitute optimal trainer behaviors in opening and later Structured Learning groups.

Outline of Trainer Behavior in Opening Structured Learning Sessions

The following outline gives the trainer a step-by-step explanation of what to do and say during the first Structured Learning session.

A. Introductions
   1. Trainers introduce themselves.
   2. Trainers invite trainees to introduce themselves. During this time trainers can ask for some additional information as a way of breaking the ice.

   Examples: — "How about if we go around the group, and each person says his name and one thing he likes (and one thing he dislikes) about school."
   — "Why don't you tell us your name and one activity you like outside of school."

B. Overview of Structured Learning
   1. Trainers explain that the purpose of the group is to teach useful skills for dealing with people, dealing with feelings, dealing with anger, handling stressful situations more effectively, learning planning skills, and generally feeling more comfortable in different situations.

   Examples: — "In this class, we'll be teaching you some ways to get along better with parents, teachers, and friends."
   — "We'll be looking at some ways to help you stay out of trouble."
   — "We'll be practicing some ways to express yourselves better to adults and others who don't seem to understand you."
   — Name some skills that will be useful (expressing anger in a way that doesn't wind up with you sitting in the principal's office, etc.).
   2. Trainers describe specific procedures for learning the skills, indicating that the method is the same as that for learning anything new (same way as you learn a sport, learn to drive a car, etc.).

   Examples: — a. Show (modeling): "We'll show you the way to do it."

        — b. Try (role playing): "You'll practice it, rehearse for
           when you'll actually use the skill."
        — c. Discuss (feedback): "We'll all tell you what you did
           well and what you could use some improvement on."
        — d. Practice (transfer): "You'll try it during the week."
    3. Trainers introduce the idea of breaking a skill down into steps as a
       way to make learning easier.
    Examples: — "What are the steps in learning volleyball?"
              — "What do you do first? Second? Etc.?"
              — "What are the different things you need to know how to
                do in order to play a musical instrument?"
              — Ask class to give steps for mastering some activity.
              — "What are the steps or parts that make up listening?"
              (Ask class for behaviors that make up a skill.)
C. Trainers discuss with group other rules and procedures.
    1. As the issues come up in the group, offer reassurance about embar-
       rassment, fear of performing, safety of group, confidentiality, and
       any other issues of concern.
    2. Trainers describe group rules regarding attendance, lateness, group
       size, time, and place of meetings.
D. With some groups whose members have short attention spans it may be
   necessary to modify or shorten the introduction. Some alternative
   methods include:
    1. Brief statement of procedures.
    2. Minimal description of procedures (e.g., show, try, discuss, practice
       description above) and then get right into learning by doing (begin
       modeling and role playing very quickly).
    3. Promise material reinforcements for cooperation in procedures.
       This may be done in several ways. One way is to assign a certain
       number of points a youngster needs to earn in order to get candy or
       other rewards at the end of the group. Youngsters are then told
       what behaviors will earn them points. Some behaviors that might
       earn points are: answering questions, paying attention, volunteering
       to role play, following behavioral steps, etc. A tally of points for
       each trainee is kept up on the chalkboard. Rewards might also be
       offered without the point qualification and simply distributed, if
       earned, when the group is over.
E. Trainers proceed to first skill, following the outline that will be used for
   all succeeding sessions.

Outline of Trainer Behavior
in Later Structured Learning Sessions

This outline shows how the trainer should act in subsequent Struc-

tured Learning sessions, when trainees have grasped the basic principles of Structured Learning.

A. Trainer presents overview of the skill.
   1. Introduce skill briefly prior to showing modeling display.
   2. Ask questions that will help trainees define the skill in their own
      language.
      Examples: — "Who knows what _____ is?"
                — "What does _____ mean to you?"
                — "Who can define _____ ?"
   3. Postpone lengthier discussion until after viewing the modeling dis-
      play. If trainees want to engage in further discussion, you might say,
      "Let's wait until after we've seen some examples of people using
      the skill before we talk about it in more detail."
   4. Make a statement about what will follow the vignettes.
      Example: — "After we see the examples, we will talk about times
                 when you've had to _____ and times when you may
                 have to do it in the future."
   5. Distribute Skill Cards, asking a trainee to read the behavioral steps
      aloud.
   6. Ask trainees to follow each step in the modeling display as the step
      is depicted.

B. Trainer presents modeling display.
   1. Trainer provides several relevant examples of the skill in use, follow-
      ing its behavioral steps.
   2. We recommend that each exposure to a skill (since a group may
      spend several sessions on the same skill) include at least the intro-
      duction and two or three modeling vignettes.

C. Trainer invites discussion of skill that has been modeled.
   1. Invite comments on how the situation modeled may remind trainees
      of situations involving skill usage in their own lives.
      Example: — "Did any of the situations you just saw remind you of
                 times when you have had to _____ ?"
   2. Ask questions that encourage trainees to talk about skill usage and
      problems involving skill usage.
      Examples: — "What do you do in situations where you have to
                 _____ ?"
                — "Have you ever had to _____ ?"

D. Trainer organizes role play.
   1. Ask a trainee who has volunteered a situation to elaborate on his re-
      marks, obtaining details on where, when, and with whom the skill
      might be useful in the future.
   2. Designate this student as a main actor, and ask him to choose a co-
      actor (someone who reminds the main actor of the person with
      whom the skill will be used in the real-life situation).

Examples: — "What does _____ look like?"
          — "Who in the class reminds you of _____ in some
            way?"
3. Get additional information from the main actor, if necessary, and set
   the stage for the role playing (including props, furniture arrangement, etc.).

Examples: — "Where might you be talking to _____?"
          — "How is it furnished?"
          — "Would you be standing or sitting?"
          — "What time of day will it be?"
          — "Where is _____ coming from?", etc.
4. Rehearse with the main actor what he or she will say and do during
   the role play.

Examples: — "What will you say for step one of the skill?"
          — "What will you do if the co-actor does _____?"
5. Just prior to role playing, give each group member some final instructions as to his part.

Examples: — To the main actor: "Try to follow all of the steps as best
            you can."
          — To the co-actor: "Try to play the part of _____ as
            best you can. Say and do what you think _____ would
            do."
          — To the other trainees in the group: "Watch how well
            _____ follows the steps so that we can talk about it
            after the role play."

E. Trainer instructs the role players to begin.
   1. One trainer (or trainee helper) should stand at the chalkboard and
      point to each step as it is enacted.
   2. The other trainer should be positioned near the actors to provide
      whatever coaching or prompting is needed by the main actor or co-
      actor.
   3. In the event that the role play strays markedly from the behavioral
      steps or otherwise departs from the theme, the trainers should stop
      the scene, provide needed instruction, and begin again.

F. Trainer invites feedback following role play.
   1. Ask the main actor to wait until he has heard everyone's comments
      before talking.
   2. Ask co-actor: "In the role of _____, how did _____ make
      you feel? What were your reactions to him?"
   3. Ask observing trainees: "How well were the behavioral steps fol-
      lowed?" "What specific things did you like or dislike?" "In what
      ways did the co-actor do a good job?"

4. Comment on the following of the behavioral steps, provide social reward, point out what was done well, and comment on what else might be done to make the enactment even better.
5. Ask main actor: "Now that you have heard everyone's comments, how do you feel about the job you did?" "How do you think that following the steps worked out?"

G. Trainer helps role player to plan homework.
1. Ask the main actor how, when, and with whom he might attempt the behavioral steps prior to the next class meeting.
2. As appropriate, the Homework Report forms may be used to get a written commitment from the main actor to try out his new skill, and report back to the group at the next meeting.
3. Trainees who have not had a chance to role play during a particular class may also be assigned homework in the form of looking for situations relevant to the skill that they might role play during the next class meeting.

SUMMARY

This chapter has sought to describe in concrete terms the procedural information necessary to actually organize and conduct effective Structured Learning groups. Trainer preparation, trainee preparation, and the sequence of step-by-step procedures involved in optimally conducted opening and later sessions have each been examined. As a further aid in maximizing the likelihood of forming successful groups, the chapter which follows focuses in greater depth on procedures and materials for trainee selection and grouping.

CHAPTER 4

Selection and Grouping of Trainees

The purpose of this chapter is to describe the development and implementation of techniques for selecting and grouping youngsters in order to enhance their skill acquisition through Structured Learning. Through the use of the methods presented, the Structured Learning trainer will be able to carry out the necessary procedures for identifying youngsters in need of skill training, assigning them to groups that will facilitate such skill-training efforts, and assessing accurately the youngster's progress through Structured Learning. Our goal is to arrive at a skill-training prescription tailored to the individual skill assets and deficits of each adolescent.

SELECTION AND GROUPING IN EDUCATION

Within educational settings, youngsters have been selected and grouped into classes using a wide variety of criteria. Bases for class assignments have historically been theoretical, philosophical, political, or economic. As Yates (1966) notes, at different times it has "made sense" to group certain youngsters together in classes on the basis of geographic location, age, sex, religion, language, socio-economic status, special needs or handicaps, and/or special abilities or achievements. Typically, once the rationale for grouping youngsters has been established, selection criteria and assessment techniques have then been developed. Selection might be on the basis of birthdate, county of residence, spoken language, I.Q., aptitude test score, or the like.

Homogeneous Grouping

In American primary and secondary education, grouping according to ability has been quite common. Abilities have been treated broadly (e.g., intelligence) or more specifically (e.g., reading achievement), or according to some combination of the two. Most often, grouping by ability is done within grade (age) level. Ability grouping assumes that reducing the range of relevant differences, i.e., grouping students together who are relatively homogeneous with regard to some ability or abilities, will facilitate teaching and learning. Thus, the aim of homogeneous grouping according to some discrete ability is to tailor the instructional methods to the (shared) characteristics of the group. In the United States, the grouping of youngsters according to abilities came into vogue in the 1920s with the development of tests that provided standardized group measures of intellectual performance. Homogeneous grouping according to abilities has been both praised and criticized throughout the history of its use. On the one hand, homogeneous grouping has been seen as the key to quality education, to occupational specialization, and to maximal achievement. On the other hand, it has been criticized as discriminatory, as based on biased selection procedures (e.g., culturally biased intelligence and aptitude tests), and as perpetuating the (socioeconomic) status quo by placing youngsters in, for example, "gifted," "average," or "slow" classes on the basis of dominant culture values.

Heterogenous Grouping

Critics of homogeneous grouping have typically championed heterogeneous grouping. In heterogeneous grouping efforts, the overriding aim is to group students who represent a wide range of abilities, interests, and/or backgrounds. This position draws its support from John Dewey's view that a classroom represents a society in miniature and that students in the school setting should be called upon to deal with a diversity of youngsters so that they will be better equipped to deal with such diversity later in life.

Combining Homogeneous and Heterogeneous Grouping

The evidence is not yet in, despite years of research on selection and grouping practices, that would suggest unequivocally that *either* homogeneous *or* heterogeneous grouping is clearly superior. As with most such debates, compromises tend to be reached, with students grouped heterogeneously for some activities or classes and homogeneously for other tasks or activities. For example, classes in social studies might involve youngsters from diverse backgrounds and at different reading or general aptitude (heterogeneous) levels, while classes in math might be structured to deal with youngsters at more uniform (homogeneous) levels of achievement.

As will be seen below, we feel it is possible to combine the best aspects of both grouping approaches in Structured Learning. Skill-streaming is, in part, just such a combined grouping process. In our approach, youngsters sharing common skill deficiencies and common channels of accessibility or learning styles are organized into Structured Learning groups. We attempt to group youngsters homogeneously with respect to shared skill deficits, but heterogeneously with respect to sex, background, intelligence, etc., so that a range of youngsters might be represented in a Structured Learning group even though they might all be relatively deficient in the same groups of skills.

SELECTION AND GROUPING IN MENTAL HEALTH

Traditional Diagnostic Approaches

The selection of youngsters for assignment to treatment within a mental health domain was typically subsumed under the topic of diagnosis. Historically, within the psychodynamic tradition, diagnosis was based on psychiatric interviews, often supplemented by objective or projective personality tests. The result was a diagnostic summary that attempted to describe the psychodynamic processes underlying and accounting for the youngster's behavior. A psychiatric diagnostic label would typically be arrived at with the intent of communicating something about the traits, states, or difficulties being experienced by the adolescent.

Further historical developments in the evolution of selection and grouping of adolescents were the formulation of typologies or categories into which youngsters, particularly those who had been considered to be delinquent or predelinquent, could be classified. As mentioned in Chapter 1, at least 24 such systems were in use prior to 1966. Typically they were based on information gleaned from a variety of sources, e.g., case histories, interviews, projective testing,

biographical data, and the like. Such information was generally unreliable and unrelated in any systematic way to specific recommen-
dations for appropriate treatment. In recent years, with the advent of
computer technology and sophisticated statistical techniques, the
diverse sources of available information concerning the behaviors of
adolescents have been more systematically and reliably combined
and utilized. As described in Chapter 1, the system presented by
Quay and his colleagues, as well as other researchers, has consistently categorized adolescents in terms of three major patterns:
aggression, withdrawal, and immaturity.

Mental health approaches to assessment have often been fraught
with difficulties, one of which is insufficient attention to situational
determinants of behavior. In assigning a diagnosis to a youngster or
in calling a youngster by a particular typological label, it was often
assumed that the youngster would behave in a way consistent with
that label across most or all situations. That is, if a youngster was
labeled as ''aggressive,'' it was assumed that he would act aggressively in most places with most people at most times. This simply is
not the case. Youngsters behave in particular ways as a function, in
part, of the situations in which they are placed.

Another point should be made about the traditional use of diagnostic or typological labels. Often the labels themselves carry with
them negative connotations—one diagnoses what is wrong, rather
than what is right, with a youngster. Not only do diagnoses and
other labels connote negative features, but they often function as
''self-fulfilling prophecies.'' That is, if youngsters are labeled in a
particular way, e.g., ''aggressive,'' they are often treated by others
as if they were ''aggressive.'' Teachers, counselors, or others tend
to be very cautious, or critical, or controlling with these labeled
youngsters. And, not surprisingly, the youngsters thus treated tend
to act in ways consistent with others' expectations (Jones, 1977).

Behavioral and Social Learning Approaches

Certain recent approaches to selection and grouping have been more
successful in avoiding the pitfalls described above. These approaches
have developed from behavioral and social learning theories. They
tend to be less abstract or inferential and more closely tied to direct
observation of behaviors. Also, there tends to be a more direct rela-

tionship between selection and grouping with behavioral and social learning approaches than with the traditional approaches described previously. That is, rather than diagnosing youngsters and then assigning them to the available treatment—often regardless of the diagnosis—behavioral and social learning approaches tend to tie assessment and intervention closely together. The intervention, whether a particular class or a training activity, is based in large part on the assessment. And the assessment is most often ongoing, so that the training changes as the youngster's performance changes. Assessment typically involves obtaining samples of the youngster's behavior in various relevant settings. In this way, relevant environmental influences are taken into account in describing the behaviors and in developing the interventions.

There are a number of ways that behaviors have been assessed within a behavioral framework. *Interviews,* in which the interviewer attempts to obtain information about the youngster's behavior and the conditions that maintain various types of behavior, are often conducted with the youngsters themselves, with parents, with teachers, or with other significant people in the youngster's life. The interview is often a useful starting point for gathering useful information for selection and grouping purposes. *Direct observation* procedures are also used to assess a youngster's behavior. The teacher or other observer (or the youngster herself) observes what the youngster does at particular times or in particular situations. This information, generally obtained in the youngster's natural environment (including the classroom), is most often coded and reported in categories of behavior (e.g., amount of time spent interacting with peers, number of questions asked in class). Although these direct observational methods have the advantage of being concrete and specific, they have some disadvantages also. Often the youngsters are aware of being observed and behave differently from times when they are not observed. While one can observe behaviors in particular situations, these behaviors do not always carry over to other situations, so that one has to be cautious about generalizing from the observation. And perhaps the main disadvantage of these otherwise useful techniques is that they are time consuming. Often, sufficient personnel are not available to observe youngsters' behaviors adequately, and if the job of conducting systematic observations is left to the classroom teacher, then the teacher may have to neglect other duties to perform the observation accurately.

An alternative to the direct observation of youngsters' behaviors in their natural environments is to simulate or stage certain aspects of the natural environment and then observe the youngster's behavior. For instance, instead of attempting to observe actual interactions with "authority figures," one could construct a simulation in the form of a role-playing task in which the youngster must interact with a (confederate) authority figure. This interaction could be more readily observed and recorded in a more predictable and standardized manner than would a similar "real-life" interaction. However, such simulations lose the spontaneity of real-life encounters and may elicit atypical behaviors on the part of the youngster.

A particular type of contrived behavioral observation useful in selection and grouping for Structured Learning involves the creation of "trial groups," such as those described by Goldstein, Heller, and Sechrest (1966). These authors suggest that one of the best predictors of how a person will behave in a group situation is to observe that person in a group situation similar to the group for which he is being considered. In Structured Learning this might be done by placing youngsters in a trial Structured Learning group for two or three sessions to observe how they perform. Are they able to maintain attention for at least 15 or 20 minutes? Can they understand what is going on? Can they remain seated for 15 or 20 minutes without disrupting the group? Do they follow trainer instructions? Can they role play? If the youngsters can meet these minimal criteria in the trial group, then their success in the ongoing Structured Learning group is likely.*

As mentioned previously, the youngster may also serve as the observer of his own behavior. The youngster might be instructed to count and record each time he "asks a question" or "expresses a compliment" or "feels angry." This type of self-observation, although clearly subject to the youngster's willingness to be honest with such recording, has a number of real advantages. First, the youngster's willingness to conduct the self-observation serves as a

---

*An additional advantage of the trial group is that participation in the group concretely begins to orient youngsters to Structured Learning procedures.

good indicator of motivation to carry out behavior change procedures. Second, the youngster has access to information about "internal conditions" (thoughts, feelings), as well as to overtly observable behaviors. Third, the process of self-observation is part of the implementation or transfer process for many of the Structured Learning skills. That is, youngsters must often be able to recognize what they are feeling or recognize certain situations that call for the use of particular skills in order to use them in real-life settings.

A method of behavioral observation that lends itself well to selection and grouping, particularly within the Structured Learning framework, is the use of behavioral checklists and rating scales. These instruments call upon the person(s) familiar with the youngster's behavior to respond to written questions that inquire into the presence and absence of both skill strengths and skill deficits. The use of such checklists is clearly much more economical in terms of cost, effort, and time expended than direct observations. The most useful checklists do not simply yield categories of deficiencies or proficiencies. If they did, then some of the criticisms leveled at the global descriptions of traditional diagnoses and typologies might also apply to behavioral checklists, since they would not point to situation-specific deficiencies or proficiencies. Checklists that are particularly useful identify situations in which the use of the behavior in question is particularly problematic.

SELECTION AND GROUPING IN STRUCTURED LEARNING

In Structured Learning, we are interested in the youngster's skill *proficiencies* and *deficiencies*. That is, we want to evaluate how well youngsters use the variety of social, personal, and interpersonal skills that will be described in Chapter 5. We wish to know not only in a broad sense how proficient or deficient they are in using each skill, but also in which situations this is true. We wish to obtain this information in ways that are accurate and specific but are not overly time-consuming, costly, or obtrusive.

The Structured Learning Skill Checklist

Our preferred technique for assessing youngsters' skill strengths and weaknesses is the Structured Learning Skill Checklist (see Figure 4). This instrument is completed by a teacher or other person(s) who is familiar with the youngster's behaviors in a variety of situations. Some trainers find it useful to have the youngsters themselves complete the Skill Checklist, thus tapping their self-perceptions, which may be at variance with adults' perceptions. Also, this self-rating may contribute to youngsters' awareness of the skills that might be taught to them in Structured Learning, which may increase their willingness to participate if they see the skills as relevant to their lives. The Checklist requires the rater to respond to descriptions of the skills taught in Structured Learning in terms of the particular youngster's use of the skill (e.g., "How often is the youngster good at using the skill?"). It also provides an opportunity for the rater to identify situations in which skill use is particularly problematic. Thus the youngster's skill behaviors can be rated and summarized, yielding a numerical value for each skill, and the particular situations that cause difficulty in skill use can be identified. The trainer may use the Skill Checklist Summary sheet (see Figure 5) to record each trainee's skill level before and after participation in Structured Learning and thus discern increases in proficiency in each skill for which training was undertaken.

Figure 4. Structured Learning Skill Checklist

Trainer: _____   Name: _____

Class: _____

Age: _____

Listed below you will find a number of skills that youngsters are more or less proficient in using. This checklist will help you evaluate how well each youngster uses the various skills. You can then use this information in grouping trainees into Structured Learning classes. The information can also be used to decide which skills to teach to a given group of youngsters. For each youngster, rate his or her use of each skill, based on your observations of his or her behavior in various situations.

Circle 1 if the youngster is *never* good at using the skill.
Circle 2 if the youngster is *seldom* good at using the skill.
Circle 3 if the youngster is *sometimes* good at using the skill.
Circle 4 if the youngster is *often* good at using the skill.
Circle 5 if the youngster is *always* good at using the skill.

Please rate the youngster on all skills listed. If you know of a situation in which the youngster has particular difficulty in using the skill well, please note it briefly in the space marked "Problem situation."

	Never	Seldom	Sometimes	Often	Always
1. **Listening:** Does the youngster pay attention to someone who is talking and make an effort to understand what is being said?	1	2	3	4	5

Problem situation:_____

2. **Starting a Conversation:** Does the youngster talk to others about light topics and then lead into more serious topics?	1	2	3	4	5

Problem situation:_____

3. **Having a Conversation:** Does the youngster talk to others about things of interest to both of them?	1	2	3	4	5

Problem situation:_____

Figure 4 *(continued)*

	Never	Seldom	Sometimes	Often	Always
4. **Asking a Question:** Does the youngster decide what information is needed and ask the right person for that information?	1	2	3	4	5

Problem situation:_____

5. **Saying Thank You:** Does the youngster let others know that he/she is grateful for favors, etc.?	1	2	3	4	5

Problem situation:_____

6. **Introducing Yourself:** Does the youngster become acquainted with new people on his/her own initiative?	1	2	3	4	5

Problem situation:_____

7. **Introducing Other People:** Does the youngster help others become acquainted with one another?	1	2	3	4	5

Problem situation:_____

8. **Giving a Compliment:** Does the youngster tell others that he/she likes something about them or their activities?	1	2	3	4	5

Problem situation:_____

9. **Asking for Help:** Does the youngster request assistance when he/she is having difficulty?	1	2	3	4	5

Problem situation:_____

10. **Joining In:** Does the youngster decide on the best way to become part of an ongoing activity or group?	1	2	3	4	5

Problem situation:_____

	Never	Seldom	Sometimes	Often	Always

11. **Giving Instructions:** Does the youngster clearly explain to others how they are to do a specific task?   1 2 3 4 5

Problem situation:_____

12. **Following Instructions:** Does the youngster pay attention to instructions, give his/her reactions, and carry the instructions out adequately?   1 2 3 4 5

Problem situation:_____

13. **Apologizing:** Does the youngster tell others that he/she is sorry after doing something wrong?   1 2 3 4 5

Problem situation:_____

14. **Convincing Others:** Does the youngster attempt to persuade others that his/her ideas are better and will be more useful than those of the other person?   1 2 3 4 5

Problem situation:_____

15. **Knowing Your Feelings:** Does the youngster try to recognize which emotions he/she is feeling?   1 2 3 4 5

Problem situation:_____

16. **Expressing Your Feelings:** Does the youngster let others know which emotions he/she is feeling?   1 2 3 4 5

Problem situation:_____

17. **Understanding the Feelings of Others:** Does the youngster try to figure out what other people are feeling?   1 2 3 4 5

Problem situation:_____

Figure 4 *(continued)*

	Never	Seldom	Sometimes	Often	Always

18. **Dealing with Someone Else's Anger:**
Does the youngster try to understand other
people's angry feelings?   1   2   3   4   5

    Problem situation:_____

19. **Expressing Affection:** Does the youngster
let others know that he/she cares about them?   1   2   3   4   5

    Problem situation:_____

20. **Dealing with Fear:** Does the youngster
figure out why he/she is afraid and do something to reduce the fear?   1   2   3   4   5

    Problem situation:_____

21. **Rewarding Yourself:** Does the youngster
say and do nice things for himself/herself
when the reward is deserved?   1   2   3   4   5

    Problem situation:_____

22. **Asking Permission:** Does the youngster
figure out when permission is needed to do
something, and then ask the right person for
permission?   1   2   3   4   5

    Problem situation:_____

23. **Sharing Something:** Does the youngster
offer to share what he/she has with others
who might appreciate it?   1   2   3   4   5

    Problem situation:_____

24. **Helping Others:** Does the youngster give
assistance to others who might need or want
help?   1   2   3   4   5

    Problem situation:_____

	Never	Seldom	Sometimes	Often	Always
25. **Negotiating:** Does the youngster arrive at a plan that satisfies both the trainee and others who have taken different positions?	1	2	3	4	5

Problem situation:_____

26. **Using Self-control:** Does the youngster control his/her temper so that things do not get out of hand?	1	2	3	4	5

Problem situation:_____

27. **Standing Up for Your Rights:** Does the youngster assert his/her rights by letting people know where he stands on an issue?	1	2	3	4	5

Problem situation:_____

28. **Responding to Teasing:** Does the youngster deal with being teased by others in ways that allow him/her to remain in control of himself/herself?	1	2	3	4	5

Problem situation:_____

29. **Avoiding Trouble with Others:** Does the youngster stay out of situations that might get him/her into trouble?	1	2	3	4	5

Problem situation:_____

30. **Keeping Out of Fights:** Does the youngster figure out ways other than fighting to handle difficult situations?	1	2	3	4	5

Problem situation:_____

31. **Making a Complaint:** Does the youngster tell others when they are responsible for creating a particular problem for him/her, and then attempt to find a solution for the problem?	1	2	3	4	5

Problem situation:_____

Figure 4 *(continued)*

	Never	Seldom	Sometimes	Often	Always
32. **Answering a Complaint:** Does the youngster try to arrive at a fair solution to someone's justified complaint?	1	2	3	4	5

Problem situation:_____

33. **Sportsmanship After the Game:** Does the youngster express an honest compliment to others about how they played a game?	1	2	3	4	5

Problem situation:_____

34. **Dealing with Embarrassment:** Does the youngster do things that help him/her feel less embarrassed or self-conscious?	1	2	3	4	5

Problem situation:_____

35. **Dealing with Being Left Out:** Does the youngster decide whether he/she has been left out of some activity, and then do things to feel better about the situation?	1	2	3	4	5

Problem situation:_____

36. **Standing Up for a Friend:** Does the youngster let other people know when a friend has not been treated fairly?	1	2	3	4	5

Problem situation:_____

37. **Responding to Persuasion:** Does the youngster carefully consider the position of another person, comparing it to his/her own, before deciding what to do?	1	2	3	4	5

Problem situation:_____

	Never	Seldom	Sometimes	Often	Always

38. **Responding to Failure:** Does the young-
    ster figure out the reason for failing in a par-
    ticular situation and what he/she can do about
    it in order to be more successful in the future?   1   2   3   4   5

    Problem situation:_____

39. **Dealing with Contradictory Messages:**
    Does the youngster recognize and deal with
    the confusion that results when others tell
    him/her one thing but say or do things that
    indicate that they mean something else?   1   2   3   4   5

    Problem situation:_____

40. **Dealing with an Accusation:** Does the
    youngster figure out what he/she has been
    accused of and why, and then decide on the
    best way to deal with the person who made
    the accusation?   1   2   3   4   5

    Problem situation:_____

41. **Getting Ready for a Difficult Conversa-
    tion:** Does the youngster plan on the best
    way to present his/her point of view prior to a
    stressful conversation?   1   2   3   4   5

    Problem situation:_____

42. **Dealing with Group Pressure:** Does the
    youngster decide what he/she wants to do
    when others want him/her to do something
    else?   1   2   3   4   5

    Problem situation:_____

43. **Deciding on Something to Do:** Does the
    youngster deal with feeling bored by starting
    an interesting activity?   1   2   3   4   5

    Problem situation:_____

Figure 4 *(continued)*

	Never	Seldom	Sometimes	Often	Always

44. **Deciding What Caused a Problem:** Does the youngster find out whether an event was caused by something that was within his/her control? 1 2 3 4 5

Problem situation:_____

45. **Setting a Goal:** Does the youngster realistically decide on what he/she can accomplish prior to starting a task? 1 2 3 4 5

Problem situation:_____

46. **Deciding on Your Abilities:** Does the youngster realistically figure out how well he/she might do at a particular task? 1 2 3 4 5

Problem situation:_____

47. **Gathering Information:** Does the youngster decide what he/she needs to know and how to get that information? 1 2 3 4 5

Problem situation:_____

48. **Arranging Problems by Importance:** Does the youngster decide realistically which of a number of problems is most important and should be dealt with first? 1 2 3 4 5

Problem situation:_____

49. **Making a Decision:** Does the youngster consider possibilities and make choices which he/she feels will be best? 1 2 3 4 5

Problem situation:_____

50. **Concentrating on a Task:** Does the youngster make those preparations that will help him/her get a job done? 1 2 3 4 5

Problem situation:_____

Figure 5. Skill Checklist Summary

Instructions: Write in the ratings (from the Skill Checklist) as well as the date on which the pre- or posttesting was accomplished. After posttesting is completed, record the difference between the pre- and posttest scores in the last column with the appropriate **+** or **–** to indicate change in performance on each skill. Since the skills are *not* equivalent in difficulty, do *not* add or average change scores for the skills involved.

	Pretest Score / Date	Posttest Score / Date	Performance Change Posttest-Pretest
Group I. Beginning Social Skills			
1. Listening			
2. Starting a Conversation			
3. Having a Conversation			
4. Asking a Question			
5. Saying Thank You			
6. Introducing Yourself			
7. Introducing Other People			
8. Giving a Compliment			
Group II. Advanced Social Skills			
9. Asking for Help			
10. Joining In			
11. Giving Instructions			
12. Following Instructions			
13. Apologizing			
14. Convincing Others			
Group III. Skills for Dealing with Feelings			
15. Knowing Your Feelings			
16. Expressing Your Feelings			
17. Understanding the Feelings of Others			
18. Dealing with Someone Else's Anger			
19. Expressing Affection			
20. Dealing with Fear			
21. Rewarding Yourself			

Figure 5 *(continued)*

	Pretest Score Date	Posttest Score Date	Performance Change Posttest-Pretest
Group IV. Skill Alternatives to Aggression			
22. Asking Permission			
23. Sharing Something			
24. Helping Others			
25. Negotiating			
26. Using Self-control			
27. Standing Up for Your Rights			
28. Responding to Teasing			
29. Avoiding Trouble with Others			
30. Keeping Out of Fights			
Group V. Skills for Dealing with Stress			
31. Making a Complaint			
32. Answering a Complaint			
33. Sportsmanship After the Game			
34. Dealing with Embarrassment			
35. Dealing with Being Left Out			
36. Standing Up for a Friend			
37. Responding to Persuasion			
38. Responding to Failure			
39. Dealing with Contradictory Messages			
40. Dealing with an Accusation			
41. Getting Ready for a Difficult Conversation			
42. Dealing with Group Pressure			
Group VI. Planning Skills			
43. Deciding on Something to Do			
44. Deciding What Caused a Problem			
45. Setting a Goal			
46. Deciding on Your Abilities			
47. Gathering Information			
48. Arranging Problems by Importance			
49. Making a Decision			
50. Concentrating on a Task			

Once information from the Skill Checklist is obtained for youngsters, they can then be skillstreamed, i.e., grouped according to
common skill deficits and trained by Structured Learning to remove
or reduce such deficits. Youngsters who are all relatively deficient in

a group of skills (e.g., Beginning Social Skills or Skill Alternatives to Aggression) are placed together. The trainees so grouped are thus relatively homogeneous with regard to their skill deficits but may be heterogeneous with regard to their age, grade, or other salient characteristics.

The Skill Training Grouping Chart

Ratings obtained from a youngster's Skill Checklist may be entered in the Skill Training Grouping Chart (see Figure 6). This chart provides a visual summary of ratings of proficiency and deficiency in all skills and leads readily to grouping youngsters according to skill deficits. The trainer should scan the charts for low ratings (1's or 2's) within the same skill group and then assign youngsters with similar patterns to particular Structured Learning classes.

There are times when it will not be possible to group students according to shared skill deficits. Instead, it may be necessary or desirable to group them according to naturally occurring units, such as school classes or residential cottages. In such instances, the group members will probably reflect a greater range of skill strengths and weaknesses. In this case it will be helpful to complete a Skill Checklist for each student in order to obtain a class profile. As explained previously, such a profile can be obtained by use of the Skill Training Grouping Chart. The trainer should select as starting skills those in which many class members show a deficiency. In such a potentially divergent group it is likely that a few of the class members will be proficient in the use of whatever skill might be taught on a given day. In that case, trainers can use these more skillful youngsters in helper roles, such as co-actor or even co-trainer.

The Skill Training Class Mastery Record

Each youngster's skill mastery within the Structured Learning class can be monitored by keeping accurate records of what the youngster does or does not do. Does the youngster participate as a main actor in the role play of a particular skill? Does she provide feedback and do assigned homework? How well is the role play performed? This information can and should be recorded on a regular basis by the trainer and is most easily summarized on the Skill Training Class Mastery Record (see Figure 7). Some trainers find it useful to have

Figure 6. Skill Training Grouping Chart

Instructions: Write in ratings (from Skill Checklist) and the date skill was covered. Ratings 1 and 2 generally indicate a skill deficit. For selection purposes, trainees having low ratings on a number of skills within a skill group should be put together in the same class.

Skill												
Trainee's Name →												
Group I. Beginning Social Skills												
1. Listening												
2. Starting a Conversation												
3. Having a Conversation												
4. Asking a Question												
5. Saying Thank You												
6. Introducing Yourself												
7. Introducing Other People												
8. Giving a Compliment												
Group II. Advanced Social Skills												
9. Asking for Help												
10. Joining In												
11. Giving Instructions												
12. Following Instructions												
13. Apologizing												
14. Convincing Others												

Group III. Skills for Dealing with Feelings

15. Knowing Your Feelings
16. Expressing Your Feelings
17. Understanding the Feelings of Others
18. Dealing with Someone Else's Anger
19. Expressing Affection
20. Dealing with Fear
21. Rewarding Yourself

Group IV. Skill Alternatives to Aggression

22. Asking Permission
23. Sharing Something
24. Helping Others
25. Negotiating
26. Using Self-control
27. Standing Up for Your Rights
28. Responding to Teasing
29. Avoiding Trouble with Others
30. Keeping Out of Fights

Group V. Skills for Dealing with Stress

31. Making a Complaint
32. Answering a Complaint
33. Sportsmanship After the Game
34. Dealing with Embarrassment
35. Dealing with Being Left Out
36. Standing Up for a Friend
37. Responding to Persuasion
38. Responding to Failure
39. Dealing with Contradictory Messages
40. Dealing with an Accusation
41. Getting Ready for a Difficult Conversation
42. Dealing with Group Pressure

77

Figure 6 *(continued)*

Skill												
Trainee's Name												
Group VI. Planning Skills												
43. Deciding on Something to Do												
44. Deciding What Caused a Problem												
45. Setting a Goal												
46. Deciding on Your Abilities												
47. Gathering Information												
48. Arranging Problems by Importance												
49. Making a Decision												
50. Concentrating on a Task												

Figure 7. Skill Training Class Mastery Record

SKILL: _____   DATE: _____

Trainee's name	Role play participation		Feedback participation	Homework		Rating of skill use in role play 1 Poor 2 Fair 3 Adequate 4 Good 5 Excellent
	Main actor	Co-actor		Assigned	Completed	

Behavioral Objectives: Participating appropriately in role playing as a main actor and completing assigned homework may serve as evidence of accomplishing the behavioral objective of mastering each skill.

youngsters record their own skill mastery on the Class Mastery Record. This more public acknowledgment of skill attainment often heightens motivation in the class.

Many educators are becoming increasingly aware of the importance of defining ahead of time those *behavioral objectives* they see as relevant for particular students. That is, teachers and trainers are being called upon, or even required by law in some instances, to define what it is that might be accomplished for each student and to evaluate accurately the degree to which the anticipated objective was accomplished. This definition and mastery of behavioral objectives is implemented in Structured Learning by planning ahead of time which skills are to be taught and then by reporting on the Class Mastery Record the level of skill acquisition the youngster has demonstrated.

Reassignment of Youngsters to Groups

The selection and grouping procedures described above are intended to aid in the formation of Structured Learning classes in which youngsters can function adequately and learn the skills being taught. Despite all efforts, however, this is not always the case. Youngsters may exhibit the management problems described in Chapter 7, which may become manifest as in-class disruptions, or withdrawal, or cutting class, or other inappropriate behaviors. Certainly, the techniques described in Chapter 7 for dealing with problematic behaviors should be employed. However, if these attempts at amelioration prove unsuccessful, the youngster may be rescheduled for another Structured Learning group more appropriate to his present behavior and training needs. Rather than constituting a ''failure,'' this first group experience may be viewed as a kind of trial group, as described earlier. Hopefully, the reassignment can be made without undue public attention so that skill training may be accomplished more successfully in a new group more appropriate to the youngster's particular needs.

SUMMARY

To demonstrate how the selection and grouping of trainees was developed, we examined some selection and grouping techniques used in education and mental health. The advantages and disadvantages of homogeneous and heterogeneous grouping in education were considered, and it was decided to use a combination of both in Structured Learning. Then traditional psychiatric diagnosis and the behavioral and social learning approaches of mental health were described. Behavioral assessment techniques were chosen for Structured Learning. The components of the assessment plan for Structured Teaching were then discussed—the Skill Checklist and Summary sheet, the Skill Training Grouping Chart, and the Skill Training Class Mastery Record. Finally, the possibility of further reassignment of trainees after initial placement was noted. In the next chapter, some procedures for teaching the Structured Learning curriculum will be explained.

CHAPTER 5

Structured Learning Skills
for Adolescents

Our presentation thus far has sought to make clear how Structured Learning groups are planned, organized, and conducted. In the present chapter we wish to turn away from concern with how skills are taught and focus instead on the Structured Learning curriculum, i.e., the specific skills taught in the Structured Learning group. We have developed 50 Structured Learning skills, falling into six content areas. These skills come from a number of sources. Some derive from our extensive examination of relevant research, i.e., diverse educational and psychological studies yielding information on which behaviors constitute successful adolescent functioning in school, at home, with peers, and so forth. Our own direct observation of youngsters in various classroom and other real-life settings is a second source. Many Structured Learning groups have been conducted—by us, by school and residential center personnel, and by others. Trainers and trainees in these groups have been a particularly valuable fund of skill-relevant information.

This chapter includes the behavioral steps that constitute each skill. These steps are the framework for the vignettes or stories that are modeled by trainers and then role played by trainees, and they are central to the portrayal. In the closing section of the chapter, the complete verbatim script for one such modeling display (Dealing with Group Pressure) is presented.

STRUCTURED LEARNING SKILLS

The 50 Structured Learning Skills are listed here in the order they will be considered. Note that they are divided into six groups: I, Beginning Social Skills; II, Advanced Social Skills; III, Skills for Dealing with Feelings; IV, Skill Alternatives to Aggression; V, Skills for Dealing with Stress; and VI, Planning Skills.

Group I. Beginning Social Skills

1. Listening
2. Starting a Conversation
3. Having a Conversation
4. Asking a Question
5. Saying Thank You
6. Introducing Yourself
7. Introducing Other People
8. Giving a Compliment

Group II. Advanced Social Skills

9. Asking for Help
10. Joining In
11. Giving Instructions
12. Following Instructions
13. Apologizing
14. Convincing Others

Group III. Skills for Dealing with Feelings

15. Knowing Your Feelings
16. Expressing Your Feelings
17. Understanding the Feelings of Others
18. Dealing with Someone Else's Anger
19. Expressing Affection
20. Dealing with Fear
21. Rewarding Yourself

Group IV. Skill Alternatives to Aggression

22. Asking Permission
23. Sharing Something
24. Helping Others
25. Negotiation
26. Using Self-control
27. Standing Up for Your Rights
28. Responding to Teasing
29. Avoiding Trouble with Others
30. Keeping Out of Fights

Group V. Skills for Dealing with Stress

31. Making a Complaint
32. Answering a Complaint
33. Sportsmanship After the Game

Each skill will now be outlined in behavioral steps. Trainer notes, which are tips that we have found facilitate skill training, suggestions for the content of modeling displays, and further comments are also given.

GROUP I: BEGINNING SOCIAL SKILLS
SKILL 1: Listening

STEPS	TRAINER NOTES
1. Look at the person who is talking.	Face the person; establish eye contact.
2. Think about what is being said.	Show this by nodding your head, saying ''mm-hmm.''
3. Wait your turn to talk.	Don't fidget; don't shuffle your feet.
4. Say what you want to say.	Ask questions; express feelings; express your ideas.

SUGGESTED CONTENT FOR MODELING DISPLAYS:

A. School or neighborhood: Teacher explains classroom assignment to main actor.

B. Home: Mother feels sad, and main actor listens.

C. Peer group: Friend describes interesting movie to main actor.

COMMENTS:

All of the beginning social skills are basic to the functioning of the group. In starting a Structured Learning group, it is useful for trainees to have a reasonable grasp of these skills before proceeding to other skills.

Like Step 2 above, many of the behavioral steps that make up the skills described in this chapter are *thinking* steps. That is, in actual, real-world use of many skills, certain steps are private, and occur only in the thinking of the skill user. When modeling or role playing such thinking steps in Structured Learning, however, it is crucial that the enactment be out loud. Such public display of thinking steps is a significant aid to rapid and lasting learning.

GROUP I: BEGINNING SOCIAL SKILLS
SKILL 2: Starting a Conversation

STEPS	TRAINER NOTES
1. Greet the other person.	Say ''hi''; shake hands; choose the right time and place.
2. Make small talk	
3. Decide if the other person is listening.	Check if the other person is listening: looking at you, nodding, saying ''mm-hmm.''
4. Bring up the main topic.	

SUGGESTED CONTENT FOR MODELING DISPLAY:

A. School or neighborhood: Main actor starts conversation with secretary in school office.

B. Home: Main actor discusses allowance and/or privileges with parent.

C. Peer group: Main actor suggests weekend plans to a friend.

COMMENTS:

We have found that this is frequently one of the best skills to teach in the first Structured Learning session with a new group of trainees. (See transcript, Chapter 6.)

GROUP I: BEGINNING SOCIAL SKILLS
SKILL 3: Having a Conversation

STEPS	TRAINER NOTES
1. Say what you want to say.	
2. Ask the other person what he/she thinks.	
3. Listen to what the other person says.	
4. Say what you think.	Respond to the other person; add new information; ask questions.
5. Make a closing remark.	Steps 1–4 can be repeated many times before Step 5 is done.

SUGGESTED CONTENT FOR MODELING DISPLAYS:

A. School or neighborhood: Main actor talks with coach about upcoming game.

B. Home: Main actor talks with brother or sister about school experiences.

C. Peer group: Main actor discusses vacation plans with friend.

COMMENTS:

This skill starts where Skill 2 leaves off. After practicing each skill separately, trainers may want to give trainees practice in using these skills successively.

GROUP I: BEGINNING SOCIAL SKILLS
SKILL 4: Asking a Question

STEPS	TRAINER NOTES
1. Decide what you'd like to know more about.	Ask about something you don't understand, something you didn't hear, or something confusing.
2. Decide whom to ask.	Think about who has the best information on a topic; consider asking several people.
3. Think about different ways to ask your question and pick one way.	Think about wording; raise your hand; ask nonchallengingly.
4. Pick the right time and place to ask your question.	Wait for a pause; wait for privacy.
5. Ask your question.	

SUGGESTED CONTENT FOR MODELING DISPLAYS:

A. School or neighborhood: Main actor asks teacher to explain something he/she finds unclear.

B. Home: Main actor asks mother to explain new curfew decision.

C. Peer group: Main actor asks classmate about missed schoolwork.

COMMENTS:

Trainers are advised to model only single, answerable questions. In role play, trainees should be instructed to do likewise.

GROUP I: BEGINNING SOCIAL SKILLS
SKILL 5: Saying Thank You

STEPS	TRAINER NOTES
1. Decide if the other person said or did something that you want to thank him/her for.	It may be a compliment, favor, or gift.
2. Choose a good time and place to thank the other person.	
3. Thank the other person in a friendly way.	Express thanks with words, a gift, a letter, or do a return favor.
4. Tell the other person why you are thanking him/her.	

SUGGESTED CONTENT FOR MODELING DISPLAYS:

A. School or neighborhood: Main actor thanks teacher for help on a project.

B. Home: Main actor thanks mother for fixing shirt.

C. Peer group: Main actor thanks friend for advice.

GROUP I: BEGINNING SOCIAL SKILLS
SKILL 6: Introducing Yourself

STEPS	TRAINER NOTES
1. Choose the right time and place to introduce yourself.	
2. Greet the other person and tell your name.	Shake hands, if appropriate.
3. Ask the other person his/her name if you need to.	
4. Tell or ask the other person something to help start your conversation.	Tell something about yourself; comment on something you both have in common; ask a question.

SUGGESTED CONTENT FOR MODELING DISPLAYS:

A. School or neighborhood: Main actor introduces self to new neighbor.

B. Home: Main actor introduces self to friend of parents.

C. Peer group: Main actor introduces self to several classmates at start of school year.

COMMENTS:

This skill and Skill 7 (Introducing Other People) are extremely important in a youngster's efforts to establish social contacts. They are not intended as lessons in ''etiquette.'' Trainers should be attuned to choosing language appropriate to the particular interpersonal situation.

GROUP I: BEGINNING SOCIAL SKILLS
SKILL 7: Introducing Other People

STEPS	TRAINER NOTES
1. Name the first person and tell him/her the name of the second person.	Speak clearly and loudly enough so that the names are heard by both people.
2. Name the second person and tell him/her the name of the first person.	
3. Say something that helps the two people get to know each other.	Mention something they have in common; invite them to talk or do something with you; say how you know each of them.

SUGGESTED CONTENT FOR MODELING DISPLAYS:

A. School or neighborhood: Main actor introduces parent to guidance counselor or teacher.

B. Home: Main actor introduces new friend to parent.

C. Peer group: Main actor introduces new neighbor to friends.

GROUP I: BEGINNING SOCIAL SKILLS
SKILL 8: Giving a Compliment

STEPS	TRAINER NOTES
1. Decide what you want to compliment about the other person.	It may be their appearance, behavior, or an accomplishment.
2. Decide how to give the compliment.	Consider the wording and ways to keep the other person and yourself from feeling embarrassed.
3. Choose the right time and place to say it.	It may be a private place, or a time when the other person is unoccupied.
4. Give the compliment.	Be friendly and sincere.

SUGGESTED CONTENT FOR MODELING DISPLAYS:

A. School or neighborhood: Main actor compliments neighbor on new car.

B. Home: Main actor compliments parent on good dinner.

C. Peer group: Main actor compliments friend for avoiding fight.

GROUP II: ADVANCED SOCIAL SKILLS
SKILL 9: Asking for Help

STEPS	TRAINER NOTES
1. Decide what the problem is.	Be specific; who and what are contributing to it; what is its effect on you.
2. Decide if you want help for the problem.	Figure out if you can solve the problem alone.
3. Think about different people who might help you and pick one.	Consider all possible helpers and choose the best one.
4. Tell the person about the problem and ask that person to help you.	

SUGGESTED CONTENT FOR MODELING DISPLAYS:

A. School or neighborhood: Main actor asks teacher for help with difficult homework problem.

B. Home: Main actor asks parent for help with personal problem.

C. Peer group: Main actor asks friend for advice with dating.

COMMENTS:

The definition of ''problem,'' as used in this skill, is anything one needs help with, varying from problems with other people to school and other informational problems.

GROUP II. ADVANCED SOCIAL SKILLS
Skill 10: Joining In

STEPS	TRAINER NOTES
1. Decide if you want to join in an activity others are doing.	Check the advantages and disadvantages. Be sure you want to participate in and not disrupt what others are doing.
2. Decide the best way to join in.	You might ask, apply, start a conversation, or introduce yourself.
3. Choose the best time to join in.	Good times are usually during a break in the activity or before the activity gets started.
4. Join in the activity.	

SUGGESTED CONTENT FOR MODELING DISPLAYS:

A. School or neighborhood: Main actor signs up for neighborhood sports team.

B. Home: Main actor joins family in recreational activity.

C. Peer group: Main actor joins peers in ongoing pickup game, recreational activity, or conversation.

GROUP II. ADVANCED SOCIAL SKILLS
SKILL 11: Giving Instructions

STEPS	TRAINER NOTES
1. Decide what needs to be done.	It might be a chore or a favor.
2. Think about the different people who could do it and choose one.	
3. Ask that person to do what you want done.	Tell the person how to do it when the task is complex.
4. Ask the other person if he/she understands what to do.	
5. Change or repeat your instructions if you need to.	This step is optional.

SUGGESTED CONTENT FOR MODELING DISPLAYS:

A. School or neighborhood: Main actor divides chores for decorating gym for school party.

B. Home: Main actor tells little sister how to put records away correctly.

C. Peer group: Main actor instructs friends on how to care for pets.

COMMENTS:

This skill refers to the enlistment of others to carry out a task and thus requires youngsters to think about division of responsibility.

GROUP II: ADVANCED SOCIAL SKILLS
SKILL 12: Following Instructions

STEPS	TRAINER NOTES
1. Listen carefully while you are being told what to do.	Take notes if necessary; nod your head; say "mm-hmm."
2. Ask questions about anything you don't understand.	The goal is making instructions more specific, more clear.
3. Decide if you want to follow the instructions, and let the other person know your decision.	
4. Repeat the instructions to yourself.	Do this in your own words.
5. Do what you have been asked to do.	

SUGGESTED CONTENT FOR MODELING DISPLAYS:

A. School or neighborhood: Main actor follows classroom instructions given by teacher.

B. Home: Main actor follows parent's instructions on operating home appliance.

C. Peer group: Main actor follows friend's instructions on fixing bicycle.

COMMENTS:

This skill concerns complying with the requests of another person. If the task seems unreasonable, it may be an instance in which another skill is needed, e.g., Negotiating, Expressing a Complaint, etc.

GROUP II: ADVANCED SOCIAL SKILLS
SKILL 13: Apologizing

STEPS	TRAINER NOTES
1. Decide if it would be best for you to apologize for something you did.	You might apologize for breaking something, making an error, or interrupting someone.
2. Think of the different ways you could apologize.	Say something; do something; write something.
3. Choose the best time and place to apologize.	Do it privately and as quickly as possible after creating the problem.
4. Make your apology.	This might include an offer to make up for what happened.

SUGGESTED CONTENT FOR MODELING DISPLAYS:

A. School or neighborhood: Main actor apologizes to neighbor for broken window.

B. Home: Main actor apologizes to younger brother for picking on him.

C. Peer group: Main actor apologizes to friend for betraying a confidence.

GROUP II: ADVANCED SOCIAL SKILLS
SKILL 14: Convincing Others

STEPS	TRAINER NOTES
1. Decide if you want to convince someone about something.	It might be doing something your way, going someplace, interpreting events, or evaluating ideas.
2. Tell the other person your idea.	Focus on both content of ideas and feelings about point of view.
3. Ask the other person what he/she thinks about it.	This requires use of listening skill.
4. Tell why you think your idea is a good one.	
5. Ask the other person to think about what you said before making up his/her mind.	Check on the other person's decision at a later point in time.

SUGGESTED CONTENT FOR MODELING DISPLAYS:

A. School or neighborhood: Main actor convinces storekeeper that he/she deserves job.

B. Home: Main actor convinces parent that he/she is responsible enough to stay out late.

C. Peer group: Main actor convinces friend to include new person in game.

COMMENTS:

In persuading someone of something, a person needs to understand both sides of the argument. Use of this skill assumes that if the other person is asked about his/her position and there is no difference of opinion, the role play should end at Step 3.

GROUP III: SKILLS FOR DEALING WITH FEELINGS
Skill 15: Knowing Your Feelings

STEPS	TRAINER NOTES
1. Tune in to what is going on in your body that helps you know what you are feeling.	Some cues are blushing, butterflies in your stomach, tight muscles, etc.
2. Decide what happened to make you feel that way.	Focus on outside events such as a fight, a surprise, etc.
3. Decide what you could call the feeling.	Possibilities are anger, fear, embarrassment, joy, happiness, sadness, disappointment, frustration, excitement, anxiety, etc. Trainer should place a list of feelings on the board and encourage trainees to contribute additional suggestions.

SUGGESTED CONTENT FOR MODELING DISPLAYS:

A. School or neighborhood: Main actor feels embarrassed when caught unprepared in class.

B. Home: Main actor is angry when unjustly accused at home.

C. Peer group: Main actor is happy when friend pays compliment.

COMMENTS:

This has been included as a separate skill for adolescents to learn prior to practicing the expression of feelings to another person. Frequently, feelings can be confused with one another, resulting in rather vague, but strong, emotions. Once the feeling can be labeled accurately, the trainee can go on to the next skill, which involves prosocial modes of expressing the feeling.

Step 1 above, involving "tuning in" to body feelings, is often a new experience for many people. Spend as much time as needed in discussing, giving examples, and practicing this step before going to subsequent steps.

GROUP III: SKILLS FOR DEALING WITH FEELINGS
SKILL 16: Expressing Your Feelings

STEPS	TRAINER NOTES
1. Tune in to what is going on in your body.	
2. Decide what happened to make you feel that way.	
3. Decide what you are feeling.	Possibilities are happy, sad, in a bad mood, nervous, worried, scared, embarrassed, disappointed, frustrated, etc. Trainer should place a list of feelings on the board.
4. Think about the different ways to express your feeling and pick one.	Consider prosocial alternatives such as talking about a feeling, doing a physical activity to blow off steam, telling the object of the feeling about the feeling, walking away from emotional situations, or delaying action. Consider how, when, where, and to whom the feeling could be expressed.
5. Express your feeling.	

SUGGESTED CONTENT FOR MODELING DISPLAYS:

A. School or neighborhood: Main actor tells teacher about feeling nervous before test.

B. Home: Main actor tells parent about feeling embarrassed when treated like a child.

C. Peer group: Main actor hugs friend when learning of friend's success.

GROUP III: SKILLS FOR DEALING WITH FEELINGS
Skill 17: Understanding the Feelings of Others

STEPS	TRAINER NOTES
1. Watch the other person.	Notice tone of voice, posture, and facial expression.
2. Listen to what the person is saying.	Try to understand the content.
3. Figure out what the other person might be feeling.	He/she may be angry, sad, anxious, etc.
4. Think about ways to show you understand what he/she is feeling.	You might tell him/her, touch him/her, or leave the person alone.
5. Decide on the best way and do it.	

SUGGESTED CONTENT FOR MODELING DISPLAYS:

A. School or neighborhood: Main actor brings gift to neighbor whose spouse has been ill.

B. Home: Main actor recognizes parent is preoccupied with financial concerns and decides to leave parent alone.

C. Peer group: Main actor lets friend know he/she understands friend's discomfort on meeting new people.

COMMENTS:

This skill is well known by the term *empathy*. Although difficult to teach, it is most important that it be included in a trainee's repertoire of skills.

GROUP III: SKILLS FOR DEALING WITH FEELINGS
SKILL 18: Dealing with Someone Else's Anger

STEPS	TRAINER NOTES
1. Listen to the person who is angry.	Don't interrupt; stay calm.
2. Try to understand what the angry person is saying and feeling.	Ask questions to get explanations of what you don't understand; restate them to yourself.
3. Decide if you can say or do something to deal with the situation.	Think about ways of dealing with the problem. This may include just listening, being empathic, doing something to correct the problem, ignoring it, or being assertive.
4. If you can, deal with the other person's anger.	

SUGGESTED CONTENT FOR MODELING DISPLAYS:

A. School or neighborhood: Main actor responds to teacher who is angry about disruptive behavior in class by agreeing to cooperate by paying attention.

B. Home: Main actor responds to parent who is angry about messy house by agreeing to do a fair share of work.

C. Peer group: Main actor responds to friend's anger about name calling by denying that he/she took part in it.

COMMENTS:

This skill refers to anger being directed at the trainee. As such, it usually requires some action on the part of the trainee to deal with the situation. Trainer should have trainee make use of the steps for Listening (Skill 1) when enacting the first step of this skill.

GROUP III: SKILLS FOR DEALING WITH FEELINGS
Skill 19: Expressing Affection

STEPS	TRAINER NOTES
1. Decide if you have good feelings about the other person.	
2. Decide if the other person would like to know about your feelings.	Consider the possible consequences, e.g., happiness, misinterpretation, embarrassment, encouragement of friendship, etc.
3. Choose the best way to express your feelings.	Do something; say something.
4. Choose the best time and place to express your feelings.	
5. Express your feelings in a friendly way.	

SUGGESTED CONTENT FOR MODELING DISPLAYS:

A. School or neighborhood: Main actor expresses positive feelings toward guidance counselor after unburdening personal problem.

B. Home: Main actor brings small gift to parent as token of affection.

C. Peer group: Main actor expresses friendly feelings toward new friend.

COMMENTS:

Although trainees initially will associate this skill with romantic relationships, they will soon grasp the notion that affection and caring can be expressed toward a wide variety of persons.

GROUP III: SKILLS FOR DEALING WITH FEELINGS
SKILL 20: Dealing with Fear

STEPS	TRAINER NOTES
1. Decide if you are feeling afraid.	Use Skill 15, "Knowing Your Feelings."
2. Think about what you might be afraid of.	Think about alternative possibilities and choose the most likely one.
3. Figure out if the fear is realistic.	Is the feared object really a threat? You may need to check this out with another person or may need more information.
4. Take steps to reduce your fear.	You might talk with someone, leave the scene, or gradually approach the fearful situation.

SUGGESTED CONTENT FOR MODELING DISPLAYS:

A. School or neighborhood: Main actor is fearful of repercussions after breaking neighbor's window and discusses fear with parent.

B. Home: Main actor is afraid of being home alone and arranges to have friend visit.

C. Peer group: After being teased by older neighborhood youth, main actor is fearful of being beaten up and takes steps to avoid confrontation.

COMMENTS:

Group discussion can be quite useful in examining how realistic particular fears are. Trainers should be sensitive to the fact that trainees may be reluctant to reveal their fears to peers. Modeling of fearful situations may help them to overcome this reluctance.

GROUP III: SKILLS FOR DEALING WITH FEELINGS
Skill 21: Rewarding Yourself

STEPS	TRAINER NOTES
1. Decide if you have done some-thing that deserves a reward.	It might be something you have succeeded at or some area of progress.
2. Decide what you could say to reward yourself.	Use praise, approval, or encourage-ment.
3. Decide what you could do to reward yourself.	You might buy something, go someplace, or increase or decrease an activity.
4. Reward yourself.	Say and do it.

SUGGESTED CONTENT FOR MODELING DISPLAYS:

A. School or neighborhood: Main actor rewards self after studying hard and doing well on exam by going to movie after school.

B. Home: Main actor rewards self with positive self-statement after avoiding fight with older sibling.

C. Peer group: Main actor rewards self by buying soda after convincing peers to join neighborhood club.

COMMENTS:

Be sure trainee tries to apply the following rules, all of which increase the effectiveness of self-reward:
1. Reward yourself as soon as possible after successful performance.
2. Reward yourself only *after* successful performance, not before.
3. The better your performance, the better your self-reward.
See Chapter 3 for further discussion of self-reward.

GROUP IV: SKILL ALTERNATIVES TO AGGRESSION
SKILL 22: Asking Permission

STEPS	TRAINER NOTES
1. Decide what you would like to do for which you need permission.	Ask if you want to borrow something or request a special privilege.
2. Decide who you have to ask for permission.	Ask the owner, manager, or teacher.
3. Decide how to ask for permission.	Ask out loud; ask privately; ask in writing.
4. Pick the right time and place.	
5. Ask for permission.	

SUGGESTED CONTENT FOR MODELING DISPLAYS:

A. School or neighborhood: Main actor asks shop teacher for permission to use new power tool.

B. Home: Main actor asks parent for permission to stay out past curfew.

C. Peer group: Main actor asks friend for permission to borrow sporting equipment.

COMMENTS:

Prior to practicing this skill, it is frequently useful to discuss situations that require permission. Some youngsters may tend to ask permission for things that could be done independently (without permission), while others neglect to ask permission in situations that require doing so.

GROUP IV: SKILL ALTERNATIVES TO AGGRESSION
SKILL 23: Sharing Something

STEPS	TRAINER NOTES
1. Decide if you might like to share some of what you have.	You could divide the item between yourself and others or allow others to use the item.
2. Think about how the other person might feel about your sharing.	He/she might feel pleased, indifferent, suspicious, or insulted.
3. Offer to share in a direct and friendly way.	Make the offer sincere, allowing the other to decline if he/she wishes.

SUGGESTED CONTENT FOR MODELING DISPLAYS:

A. School or neighborhood: Main actor offers to share book with classmate who has forgotten own book.

B. Home: Main actor offers to share candy with sibling.

C. Peer group: Main actor invites friend to try his new bicycle.

GROUP IV: SKILL ALTERNATIVES TO AGGRESSION
Skill 24: Helping Others

STEPS	TRAINER NOTES
1. Decide if the other person might need and want your help.	Think about the needs of the other person; observe.
2. Think of the ways you could be helpful.	You could be doing something, giving encouragement, or getting help from someone else.
3. Ask the other person if he/she needs and wants your help.	Make the offer sincere, allowing the other to decline if he/she wishes.
4. Help the other person.	

SUGGESTED CONTENT FOR MODELING DISPLAYS:

A. School or neighborhood: Main actor offers to help teacher arrange chairs in classroom.

B. Home: Main actor offers to prepare dinner.

C. Peer group: Main actor offers to bring class assignments home for sick friend.

GROUP IV: SKILL ALTERNATIVES TO AGGRESSION
SKILL 25: Negotiating

STEPS	TRAINER NOTES
1. Decide if you and the other person are having a difference of opinion.	Are you getting tense or arguing?
2. Tell the other person what you think about the problem.	State your own position and your perception of the other's position.
3. Ask the other person what he/she thinks about the problem.	
4. Listen openly to his/her answer.	
5. Think about why the other person might feel this way.	
6. Suggest a compromise.	Be sure the proposed compromise takes into account the opinions and feelings of *both* persons.

SUGGESTED CONTENT FOR MODELING DISPLAYS:

A. School or neighborhood: Main actor negotiates with neighbor a fee for after-school chores.

B. Home: Main actor negotiates with parent about curfew.

C. Peer group: Main actor negotiates with friend about what recreational activity to participate in.

COMMENTS:

Negotiating is a skill that presupposes an ability to understand the feelings of others (Skill 17). We suggest that Skill 17 be reviewed prior to teaching Negotiating. Negotiating is also similar in some respects to Skill 14, Convincing Others. Negotiating, however, introduces the concept of compromise, a concept that is often worth discussing before role playing this skill.

GROUP IV: SKILL ALTERNATIVES TO AGGRESSION
Skill 26: Using Self-control

STEPS	TRAINER NOTES
1. Tune in to what is going on in your body that helps you know that you are about to lose control of yourself.	Are you getting tense, angry, hot, fidgety?
2. Decide what happened to make you feel this way.	Consider outside events or "internal" events (thoughts).
3. Think about ways in which you might control yourself.	Slow down; count to 10; assert yourself; leave; do something else.
4. Choose the best way to control yourself, and do it.	

SUGGESTED CONTENT FOR MODELING DISPLAYS:

A. School or neighborhood: Main actor controls yelling at teacher when teacher criticizes harshly.

B. Home: Main actor controls self when parent forbids desired activity.

C. Peer group: Main actor controls self when friend takes something without asking permission.

COMMENTS:

It is often helpful to discuss various ways of controlling oneself before role playing the skill. The list of self-control techniques can be written on the board and used to generate alternative tactics youngsters can use in a variety of situations.

GROUP IV: SKILL ALTERNATIVES TO AGGRESSION
SKILL 27: Standing Up for Your Rights

STEPS	TRAINER NOTES
1. Pay attention to what is going on in your body that helps you know that you are dissatisfied and would like to stand up for yourself.	Cues are tight muscles, butterflies in your stomach, etc.
2. Decide what happened to make you feel dissatisfied.	Are you being taken advantage of, ignored, mistreated, or teased?
3. Think about ways in which you might stand up for yourself, and choose one.	Seek help; say what is on your mind; get a majority opinion; choose the right time and place.
4. Stand up for yourself in a direct and reasonable way.	

SUGGESTED CONTENT FOR MODELING DISPLAYS:

A. School or neighborhood: Main actor approaches teacher after being disciplined unfairly.

B. Home: Main actor talks with parent about need for more privacy.

C. Peer group: Main actor talks with peer after not being chosen for the club (team).

COMMENTS:

Also known as assertiveness, this skill is particularly important for withdrawn or shy trainees, as well as trainees whose typical responses are inappropriately aggressive.

GROUP IV: SKILL ALTERNATIVES TO AGGRESSION
SKILL 28: Responding to Teasing

STEPS	TRAINER NOTES
1. Decide if you are being teased.	Are others making jokes or whispering?
2. Think about ways to deal with the teasing.	Gracefully accept it; make a joke of it; ignore it.
3. Choose the best way and do it.	When possible, avoid alternatives that foster aggression, malicious counterteasing, and withdrawal.

SUGGESTED CONTENT FOR MODELING DISPLAYS:

A. School or neighborhood: Main actor ignores classmate's comments when volunteering to help teacher after class.

B. Home: Main actor tells sibling to stop teasing about new haircut.

C. Peer group: Main actor deals with peer's teasing about a girlfriend or boyfriend by making joke of it.

GROUP IV: SKILL ALTERNATIVES TO AGGRESSION
SKILL 29: Avoiding Trouble with Others

STEPS	TRAINER NOTES
1. Decide if you are in a situation that might get you into trouble.	Examine immediate and long-range consequences.
2. Decide if you want to get out of the situation.	Consider risks vs. gains.
3. Tell the other people what you decided and why.	
4. Suggest other things you might do.	Consider prosocial alternatives.
5. Do what you think is best for you.	

SUGGESTED CONTENT FOR MODELING DISPLAYS:

A. School or neighborhood: Main actor tells classmates he/she will not cut class with them.

B. Home: Main actor refuses to go for ride in family car without permission.

C. Peer group: Main actor decides not to join peers in petty shoplifting.

COMMENTS:

In Step 3, the reasons for decisions may vary according to the trainee's level of moral reasoning, e.g., fear of punishment, social conformity, or concern for others.

GROUP IV: SKILL ALTERNATIVES TO AGGRESSION
SKILL 30: Keeping Out of Fights

STEPS	TRAINER NOTES
1. Stop and think about why you want to fight.	
2. Decide what you want to happen in the long run.	What is the long-range outcome?
3. Think about other ways to handle the situation besides fighting.	You might negotiate, stand up for your rights, ask for help, or pacify him/her.
4. Decide on the best way to handle the situation and do it.	

SUGGESTED CONTENT FOR MODELING DISPLAYS:

A. School or neighborhood: Main actor tells classmate that he/she wants to talk out their differences instead of being pressured to fight.

B. Home: Main actor resolves potential fight with older sibling by asking parent to intervene.

C. Peer group: Main actor goes for help when he/she sees peers fighting on school steps.

COMMENTS:

Prior to teaching this skill, it is often useful to review Skill 26, Using Self-control.

GROUP V: SKILLS FOR DEALING WITH STRESS
SKILL 31: Making a Complaint

STEPS	TRAINER NOTES
1. Decide what your complaint is.	What is the problem?
2. Decide who to complain to.	Who can resolve it?
3. Tell that person your complaint.	Consider alternative ways to complain, e.g., politely, assertively, privately.
4. Tell that person what you would like done about the problem.	Offer a helpful suggestion about resolving the problem.
5. Ask how he/she feels about what you've said.	

SUGGESTED CONTENT FOR MODELING DISPLAYS:

A. School or neighborhood: Main actor complains to guidance counselor about being assigned to class that is too difficult.

B. Home: Main actor complains to sibling about unfair division of chores.

C. Peer group: Main actor complains to friend about spreading a rumor.

GROUP V: SKILLS FOR DEALING WITH STRESS
SKILL 32: Answering a Complaint

STEPS	TRAINER NOTES
1. Listen to the complaint.	Listen openly.
2. Ask the person to explain anything you don't understand.	
3. Tell the person that you understand the complaint.	Rephrase; acknowledge the content and feeling.
4. State your ideas about the complaint, accepting the blame if appropriate.	
5. Suggest what each of you could do about the complaint.	You might compromise, defend your position, or apologize.

SUGGESTED CONTENT FOR MODELING DISPLAYS:

A. School or neighborhood: Main actor responds to neighbor's complaint about noisy party.

B. Home: Main actor responds to parent's complaint about selection of friends.

C. Peer group: Main actor responds to friend's complaint about returning sporting equipment in poor condition.

GROUP V: SKILLS FOR DEALING WITH STRESS
SKILL 33: Sportsmanship After the Game

STEPS	TRAINER NOTES
1. Think about how you did and how the other person did in the game you played.	
2. Think of a true compliment you could give the other person about his/her game.	Say ''good try,'' ''congratulations,'' or ''getting better.''
3. Think about his/her reactions to what you might say.	The reaction might be pleasure, anger, or embarrassment.
4. Choose the compliment you think is best and say it.	

SUGGESTED CONTENT FOR MODELING DISPLAYS:

A. School or neighborhood: Main actor talks to classmate who has made starting team.

B. Home: Main actor wins Monopoly game with younger sibling.

C. Peer group: New acquaintance does well in pickup game.

GROUP V: SKILLS FOR DEALING WITH STRESS
SKILL 34: Dealing with Embarrassment

STEPS	TRAINER NOTES
1. Decide if you are feeling embarrassed.	
2. Decide what happened to make you feel embarrassed.	
3. Decide on what will help you feel less embarrassed and do it.	Correct the cause; minimize it; ignore it; distract others; use humor; reassure yourself.

SUGGESTED CONTENT FOR MODELING DISPLAYS:

A. School or neighborhood: Main actor deals with embarrassment of going to school wearing glasses for first time.

B. Home: Mother catches main actor necking with boyfriend or girlfriend.

C. Peer group: Main actor is embarrassed by being overheard when discussing private matter.

COMMENTS:

Prior to teaching this skill, it is often useful to review Skill 15, Knowing Your Feelings.

GROUP V: SKILLS FOR DEALING WITH STRESS
SKILL 35: Dealing with Being Left Out

STEPS	TRAINER NOTES
1. Decide if you are being left out.	Are you being ignored or rejected?
2. Think about why the other people might be leaving you out of something.	
3. Decide how you could deal with the problem.	You might wait, leave, tell the other people how their behavior affects you, or ask to be included.
4. Choose the best way and do it.	

SUGGESTED CONTENT FOR MODELING DISPLAYS:

A. School or neighborhood: Main actor tells teacher of disappointment after not being picked for committee.

B. Home: Main actor asks sibling to include him in planned activity with other friends.

C. Peer group: Main actor is left out of plans for party.

GROUP V: SKILLS FOR DEALING WITH STRESS

Skill 36: Standing Up for a Friend

STEPS	TRAINER NOTES
1. Decide if your friend has not been treated fairly by others.	Has your friend been criticized, teased, or taken advantage of?
2. Decide if your friend wants you to stand up for him/her.	
3. Decide how to stand up for your friend.	You might assert his/her rights, explain, or apologize.
4. Stand up for your friend.	

SUGGESTED CONTENT FOR MODELING DISPLAYS:

A. School or neighborhood: Main actor explains to teacher that friend has been accused unjustly.

B. Home: Main actor defends friend's reputation when parent is critical.

C. Peer group: Main actor defends friend when peers are teasing.

GROUP V: SKILLS FOR DEALING WITH STRESS
SKILL 37: Responding to Persuasion

STEPS	TRAINER NOTES
1. Listen to the other person's ideas on the topic.	
2. Decide what you think about the topic.	Distinguish your own ideas from the ideas of others.
3. Compare what he/she said with what you think.	
4. Decide which idea you like better, and tell the other person about it.	Agree; disagree; modify; postpone a decision.

SUGGESTED CONTENT FOR MODELING DISPLAYS:

A. School or neighborhood: Main actor deals with high-pressure sales pitch.

B. Home: Main actor deals with parental pressure to dress in a particular way for job interview.

C. Peer group: Main actor deals with friend's persuasive argument to try drugs.

GROUP V: SKILLS FOR DEALING WITH STRESS
SKILL 38: Responding to Failure

STEPS	TRAINER NOTES
1. Decide if you have failed at something.	The failure may be interpersonal, academic, or athletic.
2. Think about why you failed.	It could be due to skill, motivation, or luck. Include personal reasons and circumstances.
3. Think about what you could do to keep from failing another time.	Evaluate what is under your control to change: if a skill problem—practice; if motivation—increase effort; if circumstances—think of ways to change them.
4. Decide if you want to try again.	
5. Try again using your new idea.	

SUGGESTED CONTENT FOR MODELING DISPLAYS:

A. School or neighborhood: Main actor deals with failing grade on exam.

B. Home: Main actor fails at attempt to help younger sibling with a project.

C. Peer group: Main actor deals with being turned down for date.

GROUP V: SKILLS FOR DEALING WITH STRESS
SKILL 39: Dealing with Contradictory Messages

STEPS	TRAINER NOTES
1. Decide if someone is telling you two opposite things at the same time.	This could be in words, in non-verbal behavior, or in saying one thing and doing another.
2. Think of ways to tell the other person that you don't understand what he/she means.	Confront him/her; ask.
3. Choose the best way to tell the person and do it.	

SUGGESTED CONTENT FOR MODELING DISPLAYS:

A. School or neighborhood: Main actor deals with teacher who verbalizes approval but scowls at same time.

B. Home: Main actor confronts parent who verbalizes trust but refuses to grant privileges.

C. Peer group: Main actor deals with friend who makes general invitation but never really includes main actor in plans.

COMMENTS:

In teaching this skill, it is important to encourage youngsters to closely observe the behaviors of others around them. See if they can think about a person who says yes but at the same time shakes his head to mean no. See if they can think about a person who says ''take your time'' but at the same time makes them hurry up. That is, be sure to include situations in which the person is *told* two conflicting things, as well as those involving a person saying one thing and doing the opposite. In Step 1, this deciphering of the message is essential; otherwise the trainee will be unable to proceed to Steps 2 and 3.

GROUP V: SKILLS FOR DEALING WITH STRESS
SKILL 40: Dealing with an Accusation

STEPS	TRAINER NOTES
1. Think about what the other person has accused you of.	Is the accusation accurate or inaccurate? Was it said in a mean way or a constructive way?
2. Think about why the person might have accused you.	Have you infringed on his/her rights or property? Has a rumor been started by someone else?
3. Think about ways to answer the person's accusation.	Deny it; explain your own behavior; correct the other person's perceptions; assert yourself; apologize; offer to make up for what happened.
4. Choose the best way and do it.	

SUGGESTED CONTENT FOR MODELING DISPLAYS:

A. School or neighborhood: Main actor is accused of breaking neighbor's window.

B. Home: Parent accuses main actor of hurting sibling's feelings.

C. Peer group: Friend accuses main actor of lying.

GROUP V: SKILLS FOR DEALING WITH STRESS
SKILL 41: Getting Ready for a Difficult Conversation

STEPS	TRAINER NOTES
1. Think about how you will feel during the conversation.	You might be tense, anxious, or impatient.
2. Think about how the other person will feel.	He/she may feel anxious, bored, or angry.
3. Think about different ways you could say what you want to say.	
4. Think about what the other person might say back to you.	
5. Think about any other things that might happen during the conversation.	Repeat Steps 1–5 at least twice, using different approaches to the situation.
6. Choose the best approach you can think of and try it.	

SUGGESTED CONTENT FOR MODELING DISPLAYS:

A. School or neighborhood: Main actor prepares to talk with teacher about dropping subject.

B. Home: Main actor prepares to tell parent about school failure.

C. Peer group: Main actor prepares to ask for first date.

COMMENTS:

In preparing for difficult or stressful conversations, it is useful for youngsters to see that the way they approach the situation can influence the final outcome. This skill involves rehearsing a variety of approaches and then reflecting upon which approach produces the best results. Feedback from group members on the effectiveness of each approach can be particularly useful in this regard.

GROUP V: SKILLS FOR DEALING WITH STRESS
SKILL 42: Dealing with Group Pressure

STEPS	TRAINER NOTES
1. Think about what the group wants you to do and why.	Listen to other people; decide what the real meaning is; try to understand what is being said.
2. Decide what you want to do.	Yield; resist; delay; negotiate.
3. Decide how to tell the group what you want to do.	Give reasons; talk to one person only; delay; assert yourself.
4. Tell the group what you have decided.	

SUGGESTED CONTENT FOR MODELING DISPLAY:

A. School or neighborhood: Main actor deals with group pressure to vandalize neighborhood.

B. Home: Main actor deals with family pressure to break up friendship.

C. Peer group: Main actor deals with pressure to fight.

GROUP VI: PLANNING SKILLS
SKILL 43: Deciding on Something to Do

STEPS	TRAINER NOTES
1. Decide whether you are feeling bored or dissatisfied with what you are doing.	Are you not concentrating, getting fidgety, or disrupting others who are involved in an activity?
2. Think of things you have enjoyed doing in the past.	
3. Decide which one you might be able to do now.	Focus on prosocial alternatives; include others if appropriate.
4. Start the activity.	

SUGGESTED CONTENT FOR MODELING DISPLAYS:

A. School or neighborhood: Main actor chooses after-school activity in which to participate.

B. Home: Main actor thinks up activity that will earn him/her money.

C. Peer group: Main actor suggests that friends play basketball instead of hanging around.

GROUP VI: PLANNING SKILLS
SKILL 44: Deciding What Caused a Problem

STEPS	TRAINER NOTES
1. Define what the problem is.	
2. Think about possible causes of the problem.	Was it yourself, others, or events?
3. Decide which are the most likely causes of the problem.	
4. Check out what really caused the problem.	Ask others; observe the situation again.

SUGGESTED CONTENT FOR MODELING DISPLAYS:

A. School or neighborhood: Main actor evaluates reasons for teacher's abruptness.

B. Home: Main actor evaluates likely causes of parents having an argument.

C. Peer group: Main actor evaluates why he/she feels nervous with particular friend.

COMMENTS:

This skill is intended to help youngsters determine the degree to which they are responsible for a particular problem and the degree to which the causes of the problem are outside of their control.

GROUP VI: PLANNING SKILLS
SKILL 45: Setting a Goal

STEPS	TRAINER NOTES
1. Figure out what goal you want to reach.	
2. Find out all the information you can about how to reach your goal.	Talk with friends; read; ask authorities.
3. Think about the steps you will need to take to reach your goal.	Consider the order of steps, materials, help from others, and skills needed.
4. Take the first step toward your goal.	

SUGGESTED CONTENT FOR MODELING DISPLAYS:

A. School or neighborhood: Main actor decides to find a job.

B. Home: Main actor decides to improve appearance.

C. Peer group: Main actor decides to have a party.

GROUP VI: PLANNING SKILLS
SKILL 46: Deciding on Your Abilities

STEPS	TRAINER NOTES
1. Decide which abilities you might want to use.	Take the setting, circumstances, and goal into account.
2. Think about how you have done in the past when you have tried to use these abilities.	
3. Get other people's opinions about your abilities.	Ask others; take tests; check records.
4. Think about what you found out and decide how well you use these abilities.	Consider the evidence from both Steps 2 and 3.

SUGGESTED CONTENT FOR MODELING DISPLAY:

A. School or neighborhood: Main actor decides type of school curriculum to pursue.

B. Home: Main actor evaluates ability to repair broken bicycle (appliance).

C. Peer group: Main actor decides whether to try out for team (play).

COMMENTS:

This skill is intended to help youngsters evaluate their capabilities realistically in view of available evidence. This skill is often tied to Skill 45, Setting a Goal.

GROUP VI: PLANNING SKILLS
SKILL 47: Gathering Information

STEPS	TRAINER NOTES
1. Decide what information you need.	
2. Decide how you can get the information.	Can get information from people, books, etc.
3. Do things to get the information.	Ask questions; make telephone calls; look in books.

SUGGESTED CONTENT FOR MODELING DISPLAYS:

A. School or neighborhood: Main actor gathers information on available jobs.

B. Home: Main actor gathers information on where to shop for particular item.

C. Peer group: Main actor finds out what kinds of things date likes to do.

COMMENTS:

This skill often precedes Skill 49, Making a Decision. Although each constitutes a separate skill, when taken together, they comprise an effective approach to problem solving.

GROUP VI: PLANNING SKILLS
SKILL 48: Arranging Problems by Importance

STEPS	TRAINER NOTES
1. Think about the problems that are bothering you.	Make a list; be inclusive.
2. List these problems from most to least important.	
3. Do what you can to hold off on your less important problems.	Delegate them; postpone them; avoid them.
4. Go to work on your most important problems.	Plan first steps in dealing with the most important problem; rehearse these steps in your imagination.

SUGGESTED CONTENT FOR MODELING DISPLAYS:

A. School or neighborhood: Main actor is worried about large number of school assignments.

B. Home: Parent tells main actor to take care of a number of chores before going out.

C. Peer group: Main actor has difficulty balancing school responsibilities, chores, and time with friends.

COMMENTS:

This skill is intended to help the youngster who feels overwhelmed by a number of difficulties. The youngster is instructed how to evaluate the relative urgency of the various problems and to deal with each according to its priority of importance.

GROUP VI: PLANNING SKILLS
Skill 49: Making a Decision

STEPS	TRAINER NOTES
1. Think about the problem that requires you to make a decision.	
2. Think about possible decisions you could make.	Generate a number of possible alternatives; avoid premature closure.
3. Gather accurate information about these possible decisions.	Ask others; read; observe.
4. Reconsider your possible decisions using the information you have gathered.	
5. Make the best decision.	

SUGGESTED CONTENT FOR MODELING DISPLAYS:

A. School or neighborhood: Main actor decides what job to apply for.

B. Home: Main actor decides how to spend money he/she has earned.

C. Peer group: Main actor decides whether to participate with friends in a weekend activity.

COMMENTS:

This skill generally follows Skill 47, Gathering Information, to constitute the general skill of problem solving.

GROUP VI: PLANNING SKILLS
Skill 50: Concentrating on a Task

STEPS	TRAINER NOTES

1. Decide what your task is.

2. Decide on a time to work on this task.

Consider when and how long to work.

3. Gather the materials you need.

4. Decide on a place to work.

Consider where; minimize distractions.

5. Decide if you are ready to concentrate.

SUGGESTED CONTENT FOR MODELING DISPLAYS:

A. School or neighborhood: Main actor prepares to research and write a report.

B. Home: Main actor prepares to repair bicycle (appliance).

C. Peer group: Main actor gathers material necessary for trip with friends.

COMMENTS:

This skill helps youngsters overcome problems with distractions by focusing on relevant planning prior to undertaking a task. Planning, in this sense, involves scheduling and arranging materials and work environment.

INITIAL TEACHING OF A SKILL

The following is a script of an introductory narration and two vignettes for the skill Dealing with Group Pressure (Skill 42).

Introduction to Dealing with Group Pressure

Dealing with group pressure means deciding what *you* want to do when other people are trying to get you to do something that *they* want you to do. Sometimes you will want to go along with them, and sometimes you will want to do something else. All of the time you will feel best about your decision if you give yourself a chance to stop and think about your choices before deciding whether or not to go along with the group.

What you will see and hear next are some examples of young people dealing with different kinds of group pressure. In each example, they make a decision that is right for them by thinking about what to do before making up their minds.

They do this by going through a series of steps for dealing with group pressure. These steps are:

1. Think about what the group wants you to do and why.
2. Then decide what *you* want to do.
3. Then decide how to tell the group what you want to do.
4. Tell the group what you have decided.

By learning to use these steps in your life, you can learn how to make up your own mind and deal with group pressure from your friends, from your family, and from others.

Once you have seen and heard the examples, you will then have a chance to try out this new way of dealing with group pressure.

Vignette 1

In this vignette, group pressure is put upon the main actor to fight someone. By thinking clearly about the situation and what he wants to do, the main actor avoids fighting without angering the group.

Scene: Several young people converge upon Jeff, who is standing on the steps outside of school.
Main Actor: Jeff
Co-actors: A, B, C (all males), Louie
(A, B, C run up to Jeff, who is standing on the steps outside of school.)

A (out of breath):	Hey Jeff, wait til' you hear what Louie said about you!
B:	Yeah, he said he'd beat you up any time—no problem!
C:	You gonna let him get away with that?
A:	C'mon Jeff, grab him when he comes outside.
B:	You ain't gonna back out, are you?

Step 1:   **Think about what the group wants you to do and why.**

Jeff (to self):   What are these guys trying to push me into? These guys are really coming on strong. I hope they tell me what this hassle with Lou is about. I'd like to understand what they are pushing me to fight for.

Jeff: What's going on, guys? Why is he going around telling people that?

A: You're going to have to straighten him out. He's telling everyone he's going to take care of you later today.

Step 2:   **Decide what you want to do.**

Jeff (to self):   I don't like what they're saying Louie said about me. These guys want to see me fight. What should I do? I could give in and wait for him to come out, but then they would definitely push for the fight.

I could resist their pushing by just brushing it off and walking away. But they would hassle me about it later.

You know, these guys could be just trying to get up a fight. Louie's working in the cafeteria now. If I talked to him alone, I think I could straighten this out without a hassle. Yeah, I've got to see him alone.

A: Hey c'mon man—you gonna fight him or not?

B: I'll go in and get him out here!

Jeff: Hold on a minute!

Step 3:   **Decide how to tell the group what you want to do.**

Jeff (to self):   How can I tell them what I want to do? I could call their bluff, but that would only rile them up more.

I could try to get inside alone and then find Louie, and they'll let me if I tell them I'm going in to straighten it out by myself.

Yeah! That's what I'll do! I'll tell them I'm going in alone.

A, B, C: He's a chicken!!

Step 4:	Tell the group what you have decided.
Jeff:	Listen, you guys wait here, I'm going to handle this my way. I'm going inside alone to get some things worked out with Louie.
A, B, C:	We'll go with you!
Jeff:	No, you said he's been talking about me. I know the guy. If the problem is with me, he'll tell me.
B:	You gonna fight him?
Jeff:	You guys let me deal with this my way. If there is a misunderstanding, I think he and I can work it out. You wait here, OK?
A, B, C:	OK, but call us if you need help!

(Jeff leaves—goes into school—sees Louie in the cafeteria)

Jeff (to self):	There he is now—he sees me—he waved to me—doesn't look mad at all. . . . I'm glad I decided to straighten this out myself.
Jeff:	Hey Louie!
Louie:	How's it going, man! Saw your buddies running through here before, talking up a storm. What kind of trouble are they stirring up?
Jeff:	Oh, you know the guys. I think they're always trying to stir up a fight or cause some trouble!

Vignette 2

The second vignette shows group pressure being put upon the main actor to vandalize an old school building. For several reasons, the main actor decides that he'd rather not join his friends in defacing the school, and he finds the courage to tell them so.

Scene: Several young people are standing outside a store talking to each other. One of them, Mike, has a paper bag full of spray paint cans. Main actor comes walking up and hears them talking.

Main Actor: Joe
Co-actors: Eddie, Curtis, Mike, Lisa

Group:	Hi Joe!
Joe:	What's goin' on tonight?
Eddie:	Wait till you hear this. Mike just got all this great spray paint. Show him, Mike.

Mike (holding can of paint):	We're going to go up to the old school and "decorate."
Lisa:	Let's spray paint names on the wall.
Curtis:	Great! Hey, Joe, we brought some extra cans. We knew you were coming. Ha! Ha!
Step 1:	**Think about what the group wants you to do and why.**
Joe (to self):	Looks like this group is all set to go over and mess up the old school, and now they want me to go along with them. Seems like they're getting ready to leave right away.
Eddie:	What color paint you want, Joe? Blue . . . green . . . red? Hey, look here, silver!
Mike:	There's no one around there now, just a couple of old houses and garages.
Step 2:	**Decide what you want to do.**
Joe (to self):	What am I gonna do? I never did like that old school, that's for sure. But they're gonna really do a job on it. They're sure they're not going to get caught—if they do, I could be in big trouble. No, I just don't feel right about it. That old school is still in someone's neighborhood, and I think they have plans to work on it. If these guys go and paint the walls, the city's going to have to hire someone to clean up their mess. And how are the people going to feel who live in that neighborhood. I wouldn't like it if someone came and painted up the buildings where I live. No, I'm not going along with it. No way!
Lisa:	Oh! Look at this! I'm taking the silver paint. When we get there I'll spray the windows.
Step 3:	**Decide how to tell the group what you want to do.**
Joe (to self):	How do I tell them to count me out? They're all excited about it, and they're not going to listen to a lot of talking, either—though I wish I could change their minds. But, there are too many of them to deal with. The best thing I could do is tell them I don't want to do it and leave. I just hope they change their minds. OK! I'll tell them I don't want to do it because it's unfair to mess up a building like that and make problems for someone else to take care of—that's what I'll tell them!
Curtis:	OK, Lisa, you get the silver paint. Eddie's got the red, Mike, the green. I want the yellow. Joe, that leaves you with. . . .

Step 4:	Tell the group what you have decided.
Joe:	Forget it, Curtis. Count me out. You guys may be convinced that you'll get away with it, but even if you do, I don't feel right about it. Marking up a building that someone else has to clean up doesn't make me feel right! I wouldn't want anyone to make a mess like that where I live. I'd have more fun going to a movie tonight. I saw a few fellas walking down there before I came here. I'm going to catch up with them. Are you coming?
Curtis:	Who wants to see some dumb ol' movie?
Eddie:	Yeah!
Lisa:	I'll go along, Joe. You reminded me of something my parents said the other day about the old school being used for a youth center if this city raises enough money, and I'd rather see the movie.
Eddie:	Hey, you guys want your paint or not?
Mike:	If that place could become our ''rec'' center, let's lay off. What about you, Curtis?
Curtis:	Oh, man! Nobody's gonna build any youth center. You believe that? Let's hit the supermarket windows instead!
Mike:	Forget it! I'm gonna try to make it to the movie. Joe, you know what time it starts?
Joe:	At seven, I think, let's hurry!
Joe (to self):	I didn't expect to change anyone's mind. I'm glad Mike and Lisa decided to come. It sure came out better than I thought it would!

CHAPTER 6

Structured Learning In Use: An Initial Session Transcript

INTRODUCTORY SESSION

The following is an edited transcript of an initial Structured Learning session with junior high school age youngsters. The group consists of two trainers and seven trainees. The trainers' goals for this session include introducing the major concepts and procedures of Structured Learning, demonstrating to youngsters the value of such training in their own lives, establishing group norms, and beginning use of Structured Learning through the teaching of a skill. The transcript generally follows the initial session outline, which is found on pages 51 to 52.

Trainer:	Today I'm going to introduce you to something new. Before we start, I'd like us to go around and introduce ourselves since some people here know each other while some of us are new to this group. We'll go around the room, and I'd like each of you to give your name and say something about what *you* like to do in your spare time. I'll start out, I'm Mr. Johnson, I'm a resource teacher here. I've been teaching at Cleveland for three years. In my spare time I like to play the guitar and write songs.
Bob:	I'm Bob.
Trainer:	Do you have a favorite hobby or sport you like?
Bob:	Yeah! Bowling.
Trainer:	Good. (Nods to next person.)
Arnie:	I'm Arnie.

Trainer:	Favorite hobby or sport or anything you do like a job after school?
Arnie:	I'm learning to build things in the Building Trades Program.
Trainer:	Thank you, Arnie.
Co-trainer:	I'm Mr. Kovac. I'm Mr. Johnson's assistant, and I like to read in my spare time. How about you, Rosemary?
Rosemary:	I'm Rosemary. (Said very quietly.)
Trainer:	Rosemary, if you could tell us in just a little louder voice about your favorite activity. . . .
Rosemary:	I babysit.
Trainer:	Thanks, Rosemary. (Nods to next trainee.)
Curtis:	I'm Curtis, and I like to go out with beautiful girls, party a lot. . . .
Trainer:	Do you have a job to earn money so you can take a girl out?
Curtis:	Oh sure! I work at the market after school and on weekends packing vegetables.
Co-trainer:	Thanks, Curtis, how about you (looking at girl to Curtis's right)?
Lenore:	I'm Lenore . . . and (giggles) I don't know.
Trainer:	How about where I saw you yesterday.
Lenore:	Well, I like to skate.
Trainer:	Fine. Thank you, Lenore. . . . Now, the young lady to your right.
Barbara:	(Whispering) Barbara.
Co-trainer:	Barbara, could you say that a little louder. I couldn't hear you from this side of the group.
Barbara:	(Coughs nervously.) Barbara. I help my mother at the store after school.
Trainer:	What kind of store, Barbara? Is it nearby?
Barbara:	It's a grocery store . . . by the apartments.
Trainer:	I know the store. I stop in sometimes on my way home. (Barbara smiles.)
Trainer:	Next?
Jeff:	Jeff. I like to draw, play pool, watch TV.
Trainer:	Thanks, Jeff. Now that everyone here has met, I want to give you an idea of what we'll be doing. It's called (writes on

board) Structured Learning. We'll all be doing a lot of things —watching, talking, and having fun while we're learning— so I want to set up one important ground rule. (Group moans.) It's really important in this group that only one person talks at a time and that we all try to listen to what is being said. We've got, let's see, nine people in the room, and if we all talk at once, we're not going to learn anything more than what it's like to live with nine people talking at one time.

Curtis:	What if we break the rule? You going to send us to the office?
Trainer:	That's a good question, Curtis. If someone forgets, I'll remind them of the rule. If it gets so bad that the person is keeping us from what the group is working on, I'll ask you to step out of the group for a while until you feel you are ready to be a part of this group again.
	As you'll see in a minute, as I get into what Structured Learning is, it is a way of learning that depends on the participation of all the members of this group . . . so we really need everyone to do their best to cooperate.
Jeff:	(Sarcastically) Why are we all here, anyway? What am *I* supposed to learn?
Trainer:	That's a good question, Jeff . . . because *what* we learn in Structured Learning is skills (writes ''Skills'' on board).
Curtis:	Hey, I got all kinds of skill.
Trainer:	Let's take an example of a skill we know about. Bob, you said you liked to bowl, right? (Bob nods.)
Rosemary:	(Whining) That's all he ever does . . . bowling, bowling!
Bob:	I got a 175 yesterday.
Trainer:	So you have this skill, called bowling. Now, if you know how to bowl, could you teach me how to do it?
Bob:	Uh, I guess so.
Trainer:	If I wanted to learn, of course, then could you do it?
Bob:	Uh huh.
Trainer:	Now everybody, see if you can help Bob teach me, his new student, how to bowl. First question, Bob, where would you begin teaching me?
Bob:	You know the Riviera Lanes?
Trainer:	On Arbor Street?

Bob: That's the place.

Trainer: So let's pretend we're at the lanes. I know about the ball and all that stuff, right?

Bob: Yeah.

Trainer: So how would I learn from you?

Bob: You gotta practice a lot. . . .

Trainer: Would that be the first thing? Let's say I just go in, pick up a ball and drop it on my foot. How would I learn? Rosemary, do you think that Bob has to do anything with me before I practice?

Rosemary: He should explain how to do it.

Trainer: Bob, do you agree?

Bob: You gotta know how to hold the ball and step up to the line.

Trainer: Ahhh!! That's a lot clearer. How would I learn that?

Bob: I'd have to show you, I guess.

Trainer: Exactly! The first stage of learning a skill is to show the person how to do it. (Writes: ''Stages of Learning'' and below it ''Stage 1—Show.'') Now Bob, while you're showing me you would be telling me what you are doing, right?

Bob: Uh huh.

Trainer: What are the important things you'd say? See if you can say them in order.

Bob: You mean like, ''This is what you do first''?

Trainer: That's exactly it. (Goes to board, writes, ''Skill—Bowling'' and below it ''Step 1—   .'') So, Bob, what do I do first? (Holding eraser in hand) We'll pretend this eraser is the ball. I'm holding it in my hands (holding it with hands cupped).

Bob: You hold it like this. (He shows how to hold the ball.) Then you step up to the line.

Trainer: Can you show me?

Bob: Do I have to?

Trainer: Could I learn it if you didn't?

Bob: (While stepping to the line as in bowling) Look. You walk up like this and you bring the ball back.

Trainer: (Imitating) I bring it back . . . then what?

Bob: You aim and roll the ball.

Trainer:	Nicely done. What do you think, Barbara? Look like a good lesson to you?
Barbara:	(Nods shyly, says quietly) Yes.
Trainer:	So here's what Bob said I should do. (Walks back to board.) Step 1. Who remembers? Raise your hand. Jeff.
Jeff:	Hold the ball the right way.
Trainer:	Everyone agree? Good (writes in "Hold the ball"). What did Bob say the next step was? . . . Lenore, you were listening.
Lenore:	Go up to the line.
Trainer:	Right, Bob? (Bob nods.) (Trainer writes: Step 2—"Step up to the line.") Next? Curtis, what was I supposed to do next while going up to the line?
Curtis:	You should be aiming the ball where you want it to go.
Trainer:	(To Bob) How does that sound, teacher?
Bob:	Not bad.
Curtis:	Not bad? Man, that was great!
Trainer:	(Writes: Step 3—"Aim the ball.") So, the next step, number three, is to "aim the ball." Is that it?
Arnie:	No, you have to throw it . . . I mean shoot it . . . ahh (getting frustrated)
Trainer:	(Making the rolling gesture) How about . . .
Arnie:	Rolling! You roll the ball down the lane.
Trainer:	Thank you, Arnie, so we'll call Step 4 to roll the ball. (Writes: "Step 4—Roll the ball.") That's a pretty good lesson on how to bowl, isn't it? (Group says in unison assorted yeahs, uhhuhs.)
Trainer:	So the first thing the teacher has to do to teach a skill like bowling is to _____? (Points to word "Show" on board.)
Jeff:	Show you.
Trainer:	To show me, you break the skill down into a couple of basic . . . what? (Points to word "Steps" on board.)
Rosemary:	Steps.
Trainer:	Thanks, everyone, for doing such a nice clear job of showing me the skill. In fact, you all at some time or other have shown someone how to do something . . . and you were

helping them learn. . . . But getting back to our example, would I now know how to bowl if you just showed me?

Bob: You have to practice.

Trainer: You mean if no one was around, I mean, you could go home, your job as my teacher would be done at this point? I could just sit there and go . . . One, I hold the ball; second, I walk up to the line; third, I aim, and, last, I roll the ball (at the last step, trainer drops eraser on foot). And if I did this over and over, I'd learn. (Group laughs, a few youngsters say no.)

    What's missing? Bob? Before I practice alone, don't I need to try it while my teacher watches?

Bob: Sure!

Trainer: So the second stage of learning a skill is to try it. (Writes: "Stage 2—Try it.") But I needed Bob to tell me something, right? And we call that next stage of learning—feedback. (Writes: "Stage 3—Feedback.") It's when you correct someone, praise them, encourage them, or make suggestions. Lenore, what kind of feedback do you think would be more helpful for me to learn—if Bob kept telling me, "This is wrong, and that's wrong" or if he encouraged me about the things I did right?

Lenore: The second one.

Trainer: Encourage the right stuff.

Bob: I don't like it if someone always tells me what I'm doing wrong. That's what my father always does.

Trainer: Let's all keep that in mind as we learn skills in this group . . . that encouragement is really helpful when you give feedback.

Bob: Tell that to my father!

Trainer: Now, let's say Bob has given me lots of helpful tips and corrections on how I should be carrying out the steps. What do I have to do now to learn how to do this skill well? (Several students call out "Practice," "Work at it," "Keep doing it.") Remember, one person at a time. Arnie, you had your hand up before.

Arnie: Practice.

Trainer: Good! (Writes: "Stage 4—Practice.") Let's look at what we found out. Learning a skill happens by going through a four-stage process. (Points to board.) Number 1, the teacher *shows* the skill by breaking it down into steps and showing the steps for the learner to see. Second, the person who is learning the skill *tries it* by going through the steps while the teacher watches. Third, the learner gets *feedback* on how well he or she followed the steps, and last the learner needs to *practice* the skill to get it really going smoothly.

Now, all you need to know now is what skills Structured Learning teaches. Structured Learning is about what I like to call "people skills," skills that have to do with getting along with people, skills like starting a conversation, making a complaint, asking a question, or dealing with group pressure. Can anybody think of another example of this kind of "people skill"? Raise your hand. Curtis?

Curtis: Making a date.

Trainer: Asking someone for a date is definitely that kind of skill.

Jeff: Making friends. Telling someone off.

Trainer: Those are both good examples of the kind of skills Structured Learning is about.

Jeff: If we know them, why do we have to be doing this?

Trainer: That's a good question, Jeff. All of us have certain of these "people skills," just as Bob knows how to bowl, and Rosemary knows how to take care of little kids, and Arnie knows about building things. . . . But each of us is better at some skills than others, and this is a place where you can get to practice those skills you don't do too well and also help others learn the skills you do know well.

Bob: Nothing works with my father.

Trainer: It may be really hard to use a skill at home with someone in your family, but people who try these Structured Learning Skills with their friends, teachers, the principal, people in stores, or people they want to meet find that they work . . . and eventually you get really good at a skill like making a complaint, for example, and you might want to try it at home. But before we get hung up on who we need to try these skills with, let's go through an example of how we use the stages of Structured Learning with a skill I'd like to teach you today. It seems that all of us can think of *some* person or event we could become more skilled in handling.

Curtis: Like how to deal with some dude who keeps calling you names in class. That's why I'm here—right?—because I hit the new kid who kept hassling me in English?

Trainer:	Each person in here knows some skill they could use better, Curtis, and if you could avoid fights in a way that made you feel really on top of the situation, wouldn't that make you feel you had learned something?
Curtis:	Yeah, but what about the guys who start up all the time?
Trainer:	When we learn that skill, Curtis, you might be really surprised at how you can deal with that kind of hassle without having to get into a fight and get sent out of school. What if you could deal with it and not fight, yet still feel you hadn't run away from someone who was bothering you?
Curtis:	I'd like to see how you do that!
Trainer:	Well, let's get started, then. We're going to work on the skill Starting a Conversation. (Writes "Starting a Conversation" on board.) Now, this is a skill that I'll bet each person here has to use some time every day. In fact, let's see how many different situations we can come up with that you have to deal with in *your* own lives—in school—outside—at home—when starting a conversation in a good way might make things work out better for you.
Jeff:	Can it be anything we think is an important time?
Trainer:	That's right!
Jeff:	In school?
Trainer:	Sure.
Jeff:	Well . . . see, I really want to earn some money. Like more than I can make on a paper route. . . so I gotta talk to someone about some kind of job.
Trainer:	That's an excellent situation where starting a conversation is important.
Bob:	Getting someone to go bowling with you.
Arnie:	Talking to the principal about a fight that you're being challenged with.
Rosemary:	Talking to your counselor about a problem.
Barbara:	To get to know new people.
Trainer:	OK. As you can see, there's quite a list of different situations where starting a conversation would be a helpful skill to be able to use.
Arnie:	What do we do?
Trainer:	I've got a job for each of you. But first we will go through the steps that make up the skill. In order to help you, here

are cards. Each card has one step written on it. (Passes out cards.) Would the person who has Step 1 read it to me, and I'll write it on the board.

OK. Who has Step 1?

Lenore: I do. "Greet the other person."

Trainer: Right. Step 2?

Arnie: "Make small talk."

Trainer: Good. Step 3?

Rosemary: "Decide if the other person is listening."

Trainer: That's right. And Step 4?

Bob: "Bring up the main topic."

Trainer: OK. These are the four steps in Starting a Conversation. Now Mr. Kovac and I will show you how to use the steps in a real situation. Mr. Kovac will pretend he is a new kid in school, I'm also going to be a kid, and I'm going to start a conversation with him where my main topic will be to ask him if he wants to sit with me and my friends at lunch. You all watch carefully to see how I use each of the four steps.

Trainer: Hi, how are you? My name is Paul.

Co-trainer: Oh, hi. I'm Tony.

Trainer: I haven't seen you around before. Did you just transfer here?

Co-trainer: Yeah. My mom and I just moved from Middletown.

Trainer: That's pretty far away. Do you like this school so far?

Co-trainer: I guess.

Trainer: (Aside) Well, he's looking at me and answering my questions, so he must be paying attention. I think I'll ask him! (To Tony) Hey, do you want to sit with my crowd at lunch?

Co-trainer: Yeah, that would be good. I'd like to get to know some people.

Trainer: Great. I'll meet you at the cafeteria entrance at the beginning of lunch period.

Co-trainer: See you then.

Trainer: OK. That's it, class. Now let's go through the four steps and see if we followed them. Step 1 was when I said, "How are you, my name is Paul." Step 2 was asking about how you liked the school, were you new here. Step 3 was when I said to myself, "He seems to be paying attention to me," and Step 4 was when I asked you if you'd like to join us at lunch. [Trainers provide one more modeling display with different content.]

Now, each of you will get a chance to act out or role play a situation *you* choose and with people you ask to be actors with you. That's what it is to try it. (Points to words: Stage 2: "Try it.")

Can anyone think of a situation in which you would actually need the skill Starting a Conversation and in which it might be tough to get the conversation started?

Jeff: Well, I've got this new neighbor, he's about 50, and he has this neat sports car, I mean, for an older guy! Anyhow, I wanted to see if I could help him polish it or something like that.

Trainer: It sounds like you have a perfect situation in which you can use the skill. Maybe we can try it out. Does anyone in the class remind you of your neighbor?

Jeff: Mr. Kovac!

Trainer: Mr. Kovac, would you play Jeff's neighbor?

Co-trainer: Sure, I'd be glad to. (Facing Jeff) Jeff, what kind of guy is your neighbor? What's he like? Is he the kind of guy who seems to talk a lot, or does he seem pretty quiet? You see what I'm getting at?

Jeff: You want to know how to make believe you're just like this guy.

Trainer: Right, Jeff. Part of the job for the person who is helping you try the skill is to get an idea of how the other person, the co-actor, usually acts. This helps to make the role play as realistic as we can. That way, when we practice it outside the group (points to chart where "Stage 4—Practice" is written), we'll be well prepared. So, Jeff, do you have any suggestions to help Mr. Kovac act like your neighbor?

Jeff: I haven't talked to him much. He seems pretty quiet, but the one thing I noticed is that this guy *always* is smoking a cigar . . . every time I see him outside. . . .

Trainer: OK, Mr. Kovac can pretend he's smoking a cigar. Jeff, describe the scene a little . . . like where would you be starting the conversation? In front of this guy's house? By his garage? What will he most likely be doing?

Jeff: I always see him when I take my dog out before school, but

I don't have time to talk a lot then. . . . On Saturdays . . . yeah. When there's no school, he's usually outside early in the morning. I think he must go for a walk up and down the block or something. I don't know what he does it for.

Trainer: How about if we say that you go up to him while you're out with your dog and you see him on the street, near his house. What's his name?

Jeff: My mother says his name is Mr. Zachary.

Trainer: So you're going to go up to Mr. Zachary and start a conversation. Jeff, do you know how you'll do Step 1, how you'll greet him?

Jeff: Uh? "Good morning," I guess.

Trainer: OK. Do you know what small talk is?

Jeff: Like, "Nice day, what's happening?"

Trainer: Fine. You might also want to admire his car. How will you know if he's listening?

Jeff: I dunno.

Trainer: Anyone in the group? Lenore?

Lenore: He'll be looking at him and talking to him. Like you showed us before.

Trainer: Good. Jeff, can I ask you to say something to yourself out loud when you decide he's looking at you? (Jeff nods reluctantly.) Thanks. Even though you'll be doing that in your head in real life, it helps the group watching, and it helps each of us remember better when we think things like that out loud.

Curtis: Only crazy people talk to themselves.

Trainer: Actually, Curtis, saying things to yourself is a part of a lot of skills in Structured Learning, and people who handle tough situations with these skills find that it's a really helpful step. It may seem a bit strange when you first try it, but I know it will be helpful in the long run. Back to your situation, Jeff. You decided he's listening to you, and now what's the main topic?

Jeff: I ask him if he needs any help polishing his car or wants to hire me to clean his car.

Trainer: Good. Let's get the scene set up. This row here by the front of the room can be the street, and Mr. Kovac . . . Mr. Zachary?

Co-trainer: I'll be standing outside next to my new car admiring it.

Trainer: How does that sound, Jeff? (Jeff nods.) And Jeff, you'll be walking along here (shows him). Ready to try it?

Jeff: All right.

Trainer: Now one last thing. I said that each person in the group would have a job, and that job is to look at the card I gave you. Each of you has a card with one of the steps. Your job is to watch how Jeff does the step you have, and when he's all done role playing, you help by giving him feedback about how he did the step, maybe some ideas on other things he did well or could have done to make that step happen better. Got the idea? (Group nods, says yes.) To do it, then, you've got to pay careful attention and, please, hold your comments until Jeff is all done. Then we'll take the suggestions one at a time in the order of the steps. OK. Ready, Jeff? (He nods.) Start walking along the street.

Jeff: Hi! Aren't you Mr. Zachary?

Co-trainer: Yes, hello there, son. How did you know my name? I don't think I know who you are. Do I?

Jeff: Well, my mother told me your name. She knows who everyone is around here. (Looks at trainer with confused look.)

Trainer: (Whispers to Jeff) Tell him your name.

Jeff: Ummm? I'm Jeff Andrews. You don't know me I don't think, but I see you out here all the time when I walk my dog.

Co-trainer: Well, well, good to meet you, Jeff Andrews (shakes hand). You know, I thought I recognized you from somewhere. I'm supposed to walk a bit each day, 'Doctor's orders,' you know. . . . Here I've got this brand new car, and the doctor tells me I need to get more exercise . . . and that I should stretch my legs walking—of all things!

Jeff: That sure is a neat car you have. Is it new?

Co-trainer: That's what I said. Had it only three weeks.

Jeff: It sure is beautiful!! Do you have a lot of time to clean it and take care of it?

Co-trainer: Not actually, Jeff—that's your name, isn't it?—actually, I don't get much time to do that. To tell the truth, those car wash places just aren't set up to clean these lower to the ground kind of cars. Maybe I should have gotten a regular old sedan type, but, you know, all my life I wanted one of these.

Trainer:	(Whispers to Jeff) How can you tell if he's paying attention?
Jeff:	(Quietly) Guess he's looking at me.
Co-trainer:	Just seems like too much of a bother to take out the hose and soap and sponge and, you know, all the things you need to wash up a car just right.
Jeff:	Well, Mr. Zachary, I have lots of time after school and on the weekend, and I'm trying to earn some money, so would you like to give me the job when you need your car washed?
Co-trainer:	Jeff, that's a great idea! I'll tell you what. You ask your mother if it's all right with her if you wash the car for me. If you do a good job, I'll pay you $2.00. How does that sound?
Jeff:	That's terrific! How will I know when you want me to work?
Co-trainer:	I'll let you know on Thursday or Friday mornings when I see you outside.
Jeff:	OK.
Co-trainer:	I'm glad you talked to me about it, Jeff. This should be good for both of us.
Jeff:	Uh . . . (looks at trainer puzzled).
Trainer:	(Whispers) Say "Goodbye."
Jeff:	Goodbye, Mr. Zachary, and thanks for the job.
Trainer:	OK. Let's give Jeff some feedback. Mr. Kovac, how did you feel as Jeff's neighbor when he used the skill with you?
Co-trainer:	I felt real good about it. Especially in the way he got me talking about my car. I felt he was really interested in me, and I think a guy like this Mr. Zachary has got to relax and respond to a young person who comes up to talk to him like Jeff did.
Trainer:	Let's have some feedback from the group. Who had Step 1? Lenore. OK, read the step, and tell us if you think Jeff followed it.
Lenore:	"Greet the other person."
Trainer:	How did he do it?
Lenore:	He said, "Hi" and something like, "Aren't you Mr.—What's his name." (Group calls out "Zachary.")
Lenore:	Yeah, that's what he said.
Trainer:	So you think he followed the first step well.
Lenore:	Uh huh.

Trainer:	Good feedback, Lenore. Step number 2. Who has that card? (Arnie and Barbara raise their hands.) Arnie, would you read the step and tell us if you think Jeff followed it?
Arnie:	"Make small talk." . . . Uh, yeah!
Trainer:	Yes, you think what?
Arnie:	That he did it.
Trainer:	How did you know? I mean, what did he do that you knew it was small talk?
Arnie:	He said stuff like, "That's a neat car you got there."
Trainer:	Thank you, Arnie. You were paying attention really well. Who else had Step 2? Barbara, do you remember any other small talk, or do you have any suggestions on how Jeff could have improved this step?
Barbara:	He said something about seeing that man in the mornings when he walked his dog . . . I don't remember anything else, though.
Trainer:	Good point, Barbara. So Jeff had a couple of things to say after he greeted Mr. Zachary.
Rosemary:	(Out of turn) Jeff always has too much to say.
Trainer:	Rosemary, you'll get a turn soon. On to Step number 3. Who had that one? (Rosemary and Curtis raise their hands.) Rosemary, now's the time for you to let the group know what you saw for Step 3. Can you read us Step 3?
Rosemary:	Step number 3, . . . "Decide if the other person is listening."
Trainer:	Did Jeff do that?
Rosemary:	Yeah, after you said something to him, he said, "I think he's listening to me" or something like it.
Trainer:	Good observation, Rosemary. Remember I said we would coach you through the role play, and I reminded Jeff to say something out loud about deciding if Mr. Kovac, or Mr. Zachary, was really listening? Curtis, you also had that step, right?
Curtis:	I agree with what Rosemary said. But I still think it's weird to talk out loud when you're thinking.
Trainer:	I guess it is strange at first, Curtis. OK. Now the last step, Step 4—that's the clincher. Who has that one? (Bob raises his hand.) Bob, would you read Step 4 for us?
Bob:	It's on the board.

Trainer:	Bob, it helps us remember it better each time we hear it. OK?
Bob:	Yeah. "Bring up the main topic."
Trainer:	Did Jeff do that, Bob?
Bob:	When he said he'd wash the car, because he was trying to earn some cash.
Trainer:	Good, Bob. Do you think he said it well? I mean, was it said in a nice way . . . a way that helped get a good response from Mr. Zachary?
Bob:	I guess so. Old Mr. Zachary gave him the job, that's for sure.
Trainer:	I agree with you completely, Bob. Jeff was smiling at Mr. Zachary and he talked in a pleasant, friendly way. . . . Here's a bonus question for the whole group: What's one other important thing that Jeff did when he brought up the main topic? (Group is quiet.) When he was standing in front of Mr. Zachary he talked clearly, he was friendly, he got his idea across, but there was something in the way he was standing and talking. . . . Lenore, did you catch it, I gave you a hint as I just went through the motions in front of Mr. Kovac.
Lenore:	You were looking at him! Right, is that it?
Trainer:	You got it. Anyone else catch that? (Several hands go up.) You guys are really getting good at this now. So when you do talk with someone at any time, it's a good idea to be looking at the person. Mr. Kovac, how did that make you feel?
Co-trainer:	Well, I noticed that at first Jeff was looking down, and I was going to say something, but as I looked at him when I talked, it seemed like he was sharp enough to pick up on it, and he looked right at me from then on. It made me feel much better—like I could believe him. You know what I'm trying to get at?
Trainer:	(Looks at group.) Arnie, you look like you have an idea. Do you want to share it?
Arnie:	Nothing much, but I was remembering that my parents always remind me to look at people when I talk to them. They say it makes people trust you more.
Trainer:	Do you agree, now?
Arnie:	I guess so.
Trainer:	Good. Thanks for sharing that advice with us, Arnie. I think

it really works into what we're doing with this skill and will come in handy with a lot of the skills we cover. Jeff, I guess the group has already told you, but I'll say it again. You did a really good job following the steps for starting a conversation. Especially with it being the first role play. Do you have anything to add, Jeff, about what the group has said? How do you think you did?

Jeff: I guess I did OK. I liked that Step 2, "small talk." It really helped.

Trainer: OK. We have enough time left for one more person to role play the skill. Next time, we'll be able to get right into this skill, and each of you can think about what kind of situation you want to try it in. Maybe you'll see something—an opportunity in school, at home, outside.

Curtis: Can we practice it today, I mean, outside? If something comes up, and I start a conversation. Can I check off that I did the homework?

Trainer: You should see how many situations you find where you need to use this skill, Curtis, and if you've got to start a conversation, then you should try it using these steps. Now what I'd like you to do with those situations you come up with is to bring them in and use them for role playing. I'd like you each to look for situations where starting a conversation might be difficult or tough. The homework, though, is something we plan on *after* you've had a chance to role play it in class, so you're sure to have the steps down pat. So you get to use the skill in those situations you find difficult.

Curtis: But I got to wait, huh?

Trainer: Only until you have had your chance to role play. Would someone else like to try the skill now?

Curtis: OK.

Trainer: OK, Curtis. Do you have a situation in mind? One where you really need to start a conversation?

Curtis: (Points to his suggestion on the board, "selling something.") That's the one I thought of . . . selling something!

Trainer: Is a situation coming up where you need to sell something?

Curtis: I have these raffle tickets for the basketball team that I have to sell. I've never sold tickets before, and it's hard to know what to say.

Trainer: Curtis, you picked a good situation, since every class in this

	school is raising money by selling something. Now who would you be selling them to?
Curtis:	Oh, neighbors or friends. Lenore can be some lady whose door I knock on.
Trainer:	How about it Lenore? Would you help us out and play one of Curtis's neighbors?
Lenore:	Oh, I guess so.
Trainer:	(Escorts her to front of room.) Now, Curtis, how about if Lenore comes to the door right over here? We can make believe that the blackboard is the door and you can knock on it. Look at the steps again. (Points to the steps on the board.) What should Lenore's name be?
Curtis:	Hmmmm? Let's see. How about Mrs. Collucci. She lives next door.
Trainer:	Good. So, Lenore, you are one of Curtis's neighbors. Your name is Mrs. Collucci. (Looking at Curtis.) Tell us about this person Lenore is going to play.
Curtis:	She's in her 40s. I never really talked to her, so I can't tell you what she's like. I know she talks a lot.
Trainer:	That makes it a bit harder, Curtis, when you don't know what a person is like. Curtis, how would you greet her so she'll pay attention when you try to sell her the raffle ticket? Let's review the steps. Your greeting? (Points to the board.)
Curtis:	"How ya doin' today, ma'm? My name is Curtis."
Trainer:	Good! Now the small talk. (Points.)
Curtis:	"Nice day today."
Trainer:	Then? (Points.)
Curtis:	Now I gotta see if she's listenin' to me, and then I give her my sales pitch. . . .
Trainer:	Sounds good! Now, for the rest of the group, everyone else trade cards with the person next to you. Good! Mr. Kovac, how about if you coach Lenore and Curtis? I'll be right here to help you out if you need it. Lenore, remember that the real neighbor talks a lot. Ready to start it out? (Curtis and Lenore nod. Trainer whispers to Curtis to knock on the door.)
Curtis:	Knock, knock.
Lenore:	Just a minute! Hello, young man.

Curtis: Hello madam, uh, ma'm, uh, my name is Curtis. I live next door. I go to Cleveland Junior High.

Lenore: Oh, yes, I pass the school on my way to the bus stop every day. In fact I am getting ready to leave for work in, ummm, about an hour.

Curtis: That's nice. (Looks at trainer.)

Trainer: Ask her where she works.

Curtis: Uhhh, I mean, where is it that you work . . . if you don't mind me askin'.

Lenore: What should I say? (Looks at co-trainer.)

Co-trainer: Make up a place.

Lenore: Over at the Fireside Restaurant.

Curtis: (Looks back at trainer, who points at Step 3. Mumbles, real soft.) Yeah, she's . . . lookin at me.

Lenore: I have to be hurrying along now.

Curtis: Uh . . . just a minute more, if you could. See, I'm selling these raffle tickets to raise money for my ninth-grade basketball team. You could win a prize—the prizes are listed here (points). Would you like to buy one from me?

Lenore: OK, I guess it's for a good cause.

Curtis: Thanks for helping me out.

Trainer: Good job, both of you. Lenore, how did you feel as his neighbor about how well he started a conversation?

Lenore: Well, I guess it was good. I was so nervous I didn't really concentrate on what Curtis was doing.

Trainer: Lenore, I know what you mean. Sometimes the part of the co-actor is the hardest one to do. After all, you don't even have any steps to follow. Would you be likely to listen and talk to someone who started a conversation in the way Curtis just did?

Lenore: Yeah, he did pretty good.

Trainer: Let's talk about how Curtis followed the steps. Who has the card for Step 1? (At this point, the group goes around and comments on how Curtis followed the steps.)

               Well, Curtis, you sure got a lot of good comments. I thought you handled the small talk especially well. You were friendly, but not too personal. Curtis, how do you think you did?

Curtis: I guess it was OK. I think I stumbled over a few words.

Trainer: I guess nobody noticed it, though. I know I didn't. Lenore, I wanted to tell you that you did a fine job as the neighbor.

Lenore: Thanks, it was kind of fun.

Trainer: I think you are all catching on well to how to use the steps of this skill . . . and it seems that you feel it really does come in handy. Next time we get together, we'll begin with a review of the steps. Mr. Kovac and I will show you some more examples of this skill to refresh your idea of how the steps are used, and we'll be able to get to everyone else, so each of you can get a chance to role play. Think about situations you might want to try, or you could use the suggestions you made at the beginning of this period. I'll save that list.

Jeff: I want to try it out on that guy, the real Mr. Zachary, tomorrow. Can I do it?

Trainer: OK, Jeff. Here is a copy of the Homework Report. Put your name here, and I'll sign here (writes in). Why don't the rest of you take a Homework Report and follow along as Jeff fills his out. We'll go over Jeff's Homework Report next time and perhaps have some of the rest of the class do some homework then. Write ''Starting a Conversation'' here (points to proper space). Fine, put the four steps in the space here.

Jeff: What do I write for ''Where will you try the skill''?

Trainer: Jeff, where would be the place, like . . .

Jeff: Out front of my house!

Trainer: That's it. Next, ''With whom will you try the skill?'' Write in his name. And fifth, ''When will you try the skill?''

Jeff: In the morning before school tomorrow, if he's out there.

Trainer: That's a good plan. Do you all see how this is set up? Jeff has the skill, the steps, where he'll try it, who he'll try it with, and when—all on the front of his Homework Report. He should answer the bottom four questions as soon as he can after he tries it out with Mr. Zachary. You even get to rate yourself for the third question. You can also write down some ideas for other places and people with whom you could try the skill.

Jeff: But what if the guy won't talk to me?

Trainer: I can understand your concern, Jeff, because we all wonder how the people out there are going to respond to us. I can

tell you two things that have helped a lot of people trying
something new. One of the things to remember is that this is
just a plan. Things can change. You can see someone at a
different time, or he might be in a bad mood. All kinds of
things can change. But if the situation is at all like what you
planned, try using the skill as carefully and with all the confidence you can work up, just like we did today. Even though
you are a little unsure of yourself, if you use the steps correctly, he'll probably talk with you. You know what I mean?
(Group says, "Yeah.")

Sometimes, though, even when you try your best, people
still give you the cold shoulder. I guess we have to understand that some people just won't change, no matter how we
treat them. All you can say at that point is that you did your
best. Does that make sense to you, Jeff?

Jeff: I guess so. I'll give it a good try.

Trainer: That's all we have time for today. I'll see you all tomorrow.
               Class dismissed.

SECOND SESSION

In this session, it is extremely important to review and reinforce the
concepts introduced in the initial session. We recommend that trainers briefly repeat the major Structured Learning concepts and procedures prior to working on a skill. The trainer might open the class
with the following comments.

"Who remembers the four stages of Structured Learning?"

"Which stage comes first?"

"What do you do next?"

Next, if homework has been assigned in the previous session, the
trainers should elicit a report of how the trainees did in carrying out
their assignments. It is extremely important to generously praise all
attempts at doing homework, particularly in these early stages.
Trainees who have not done their assigned homework should be re-
minded of the importance of such assignments and told to be sure to
do them before the next class. The trainer must be sensitive, however, to trainees who are having difficulty with or are reluctant to do
their assigned work. Such difficulties may reflect any one of a number of factors (insufficient classroom rehearsal, inappropriate choice
of a real-life setting for trying out the skill, lack of opportunity to try

the skill, etc.). Trainers may find it useful in such cases to have trainees re-rehearse incomplete assignments. Re-role playing of completed assignments can also be useful in highlighting successes or difficulties trainees may be having in their transfer efforts.

After homework has been discussed and/or re-role played, trainers should direct the discussion to the skill being covered during that session. Whether the skill is new or a continuation of one from the previous session, a minimum of two modeling displays should be presented. If at all possible, content of such displays should be different from that of the previous session.

Following the modeling displays, trainers should engage trainees in a discussion of skill use and then in role playing. Following the elicitation of feedback, homework is assigned to those trainees who have served as main actors in role playing and feel ready to try the skill outside of the classroom.

THIRD AND LATER SESSIONS

The format described above is recommended for all subsequent Structured Learning sessions. As trainees become more proficient in skill acquisition and usage, more classroom time can be spent on issues of transfer to real-life skill use.

ABBREVIATED STRUCTURED LEARNING SESSIONS

In an effort to tailor Structured Learning training to the needs of various trainee groups, it is often useful and necessary to shorten, simplify, or otherwise modify the training procedures. Specifically, we are concerned here with youngsters with short attention spans, limited ability to assimilate even moderately abstract concepts, or other problems that curtail their ability to attend, concentrate, and perform for a full classroom period.

We recommend to the trainers of such youngsters that classroom time be shortened to 15 or 20 minutes and perhaps be scheduled at more frequent intervals. In addition, lengthy discussions and introductions of new material should be avoided. Instead, trainees should be quickly engaged in observing brief modeling displays, participating in role playing, etc. We have found that such changes in procedures facilitate the learning of skills by these types of trainees.

The beginning of an initial session of this type is illustrated below.

Trainer 1:   I'm Mr. Johnson.

Trainer 2:   I'm Mr. Kovac. We're going to do something new today. We're going to show you (writes "show you" on board) how to start a conversation by following four steps (lists steps on board and has trainees read steps aloud).

Trainer 1:   After we show you how to start a conversation in a way that makes other people want to listen to you, each of you will get a chance to try (writes "try" on board) doing what we did.

Trainer 2:   Then after you try it out, we'll all make helpful suggestions or corrections on how you did. This is called feedback (writes "feedback" on board). Finally, you'll each get a chance to practice how to start a conversation outside this room (writes "practice" on board). OK, let's get started.

SUMMARY

The value of modeling as an aid to learning has been stressed throughout this book, and the illustrative protocol of an initial Structured Learning session contained in this chapter is intended to be just this type of learning aid. As noted earlier, the trainer behavior depicted generally follows the Initial Session Outline, and the trainees' behavior in the protocol corresponds in large measure to what may be anticipated to actually occur in many opening sessions. As a further aid to trainer effectiveness, the chapter that follows provides illustrative examples of an array of management problems that may occur in Structured Learning groups and that, if not resolved, may interfere with trainee skill development.

CHAPTER 7

Management of Problem Behavior in a Structured Learning Group

One of the major challenges to the Structured Learning trainer, or any trainer of adolescents, is maintaining attention and keeping any problem behavior under control. In this chapter, we will identify a variety of problem behaviors and will describe a number of techniques useful in dealing with the management of such behaviors within a Structured Learning group. Trainers are likely to find that these techniques are also useful in a broad range of teaching situations, and we certainly advocate their use when appropriate in groups and classes other than Structured Learning groups.

Structured Learning is primarily a didactic group technique that is highly task oriented. Each Structured Learning session has a particular goal (the learning of a skill) and a plan for achieving that goal (modeling, role playing, feedback, and transfer training). Thus, in this context, a management problem is any behavior or activity that prevents the group from working toward the achievement of its goal. This is not to say that acknowledgment of youngsters' feelings, sensitivity to their needs, or awareness of group dynamics should be ignored. Quite the contrary: in the repertoire of behavioral management techniques we are about to describe, the trainer must show a full appreciation of each individual trainee in order to appropriately select and use a technique in a manner that is conducive to the trainee's in-class attention to relevant material, retention of such material, and later reproduction in real-life settings.

As the reader is well aware, the major thrust of Structured Learning is to teach those useful, prosocial skills in which trainees are deficient. From a classroom management perspective, however, trainees may be deficient in certain verbal or other skills that they need in class in order to participate in just those procedures (modeling, role playing, etc.) that will enable them to learn the skills being taught.

Management problems may be divided into two major categories: *behavioral excesses* and *behavioral deficiencies*. Mann (1972) defines a behavioral excess as ''any child's behavior whose rates of occurrence exceed socially defined standards of acceptability, desirability, or appropriateness within a given context'' (p. 459). In a Structured Learning class, behavioral excesses are those behaviors that actively interfere with or intrude upon the learning process. Some of the major excessive behaviors which have been described in the educational and psychological literature are now listed.

1. Hyperactivity (e.g., getting out of chair at inappropriate times, running around classroom)

2. Aggressive or impulsive behavior (e.g., hitting classmates, yelling at teacher)

3. General disruption (e.g., interruption of ongoing activity, talking out of turn, teasing of class members, use of profanity)

4. Crying or temper tantrums

5. Dependency (e.g., seeking excessive attention or approval)

Although youngsters exhibiting excessive behaviors are also deficient in more appropriate, prosocial behaviors, the trainer certainly must be able to control excessive behaviors like those just mentioned for the teaching of prosocial behaviors to go on.

As mentioned in Chapter 1, behavioral deficiencies refer to the absence or weakness in an individual's behavioral repertoire of prosocial or developmentally appropriate behaviors. The following list presents some of the major behavioral deficiencies described in the literature which pose classroom management problems that may interfere with the learning process.

1. Inattentiveness (e.g., daydreaming)

2. Isolation (e.g., unwillingness or inability to join group discussions or activities)

3. Negativism (e.g., refusing to participate, undermining ongoing activity, cutting class, or leaving while class is in progress)

4. Apathy (e.g., lack of care about quality of work, passivity)

5. Anxiety (e.g., fearfulness, afraid to speak in group)

6. Verbal inadequacies

7. Lack of self-confidence (e.g., downgrading of one's own performance)

In Chapter 1 you were introduced to a tripartite classification of behavior disorders in adolescents: aggressive, withdrawn, and immature. Youngsters in each of these categories may exhibit classroom behaviors that are management problems of an excessive nature or a deficient nature.

Once the trainer has identified a management problem, the task becomes one of selecting a technique that will foster more appropriate classroom behavior. We do not propose that only certain techniques should be used with certain kinds of problematic behaviors. While it would be reassuring to match a particular remediation technique with each of the above management problems, research currently available does not provide us with empirical support for such matching. At best, clinical and research literature describes a range of techniques that fall into three general categories:

1. Behavior modification techniques. These methods are ones based on principles of reinforcement and have typically been used in the remediation of excessive behavior and the shaping of infrequent behavior.

2. Instructional techniques. These methods provide the trainee with specific, concrete instructions regarding expected classroom behavior. They have been particularly useful in correcting deficient behavior and teaching new, in-class behavior.

3. Relationship-based techniques. These methods help to create a supportive atmosphere conducive to learning and performance and are frequently used in conjunction with both behavior modification and instructional methods.

In the remainder of this chapter, we will describe and illustrate each of these three types of management techniques for use in Structured Learning groups. We have attempted to define each technique behaviorally, thus giving the Structured Learning trainer specific information regarding what to say and/or do in order to effect the desired change in behavior.

BEHAVIOR MODIFICATION TECHNIQUES

Increasing Desirable Behavior

Reinforcement

In Chapter 2, we discussed the importance of reinforcement as a powerful tool in maintaining newly learned behaviors in a Structured Learning group. Similarly, reinforcement is the trainer's most potent behavior management technique, particularly for increasing the use of infrequent but desirable behaviors. These infrequent behaviors might include such things as coming to Structured Learning meetings, paying attention, speaking, volunteering for role playing, and participation in group discussions or feedback.

In order to make the use of reinforcement most effective, the rules described on pages 25 to 29 should be applied. In addition, the literature on the types and uses of reinforcement provides us with a number of additional, useful techniques for modifying the behavior of difficult-to-manage Structured Learning group members.

Material Reinforcement. Material reinforcement refers to the provision of tangible rewards for desirable behavior. Such rewards may be in the form of food, money, privileges, or tokens (points, credits) that can be exchanged for desirable rewards. In choosing to use these forms of reinforcement, the trainer must be alert to the need to select materials that are indeed rewarding to the trainee. What the trainer sees as rewarding may not always be valued by a particular youngster. Thus, it is frequently useful to offer a selection of rewards from which youngsters can choose. In a classroom setting, trainers can easily draw upon such a selection of desirable activities (time off, sports) as well as strictly tangible items (candy, comic books).

EXAMPLE

In a group of particularly active, aggressive, and sports-minded trainees, one trainer decided to use a token system in which a certain number of tokens could be exchanged for extra time in the gym after school (worked out beforehand with the physical education teacher). The token exchange was printed on a large sheet of paper and tacked up where it was easily visible during Structured Learning classes.

How To Earn Tokens

Doing homework = 2 tokens

Volunteering to role play = 2 tokens

Giving feedback = 1 token

Asking questions = 1 token

Helping someone = 1 token

1 hour of gym time = 20 tokens

(Maximum tokens earned per class = 10)

Often youngsters will be willing to engage in behaviors that the trainer wants when the reward for doing so is permission for them to engage in behaviors or activities at a later time that they themselves prefer to do. This exchange approach is sometimes referred to as the Premack principle. Andrews (1970–1971) found this technique particularly useful in bringing about a decrease in the disruptive behavior of culturally deprived, low-performing seventh graders. Similarly, Nolan, Kunzelmann, and Haring (1967) demonstrated the usefulness of the Premack principle in improving academic performance of learning-disabled junior high school students.

EXAMPLE

One Structured Learning trainer used the Premack principle to channel a class of severely emotionally disturbed youngsters into productive activity almost instantly. When the students entered the classroom, they noticed some videotape equipment in the front of the room. They gathered around the equipment and asked the trainer if they could watch themselves on TV. The trainer responded: ''I have a lesson prepared today on the skill of Self-control. I will videotape the class. If we can get through the class lesson with a minimum of disruption, I will stop the class early, and we can watch ourselves on the TV.''

Social Reinforcement. This refers to the giving of praise, approval, and attention (by the trainer as well as peers) for those behaviors we wish the youngster to increase. The effectiveness of social reinforcement in a classroom setting for increasing desirable behaviors is well supported by research. For example, Becker, Madsen, Arnold, and Thomas (1967) found that teacher praise and attention to the appropriate behavior of elementary school children was effective in increasing such appropriate behaviors in children who were exhibiting inappropriate behavior. Solomon and Wahler (1973) demonstrated a similar effect in sixth graders, with peers serving as the reinforcers of appropriate classroom behavior.

EXAMPLE

In a new Structured Learning group, the trainees were learning the skill Starting a Conversation. One of the withdrawn girls, Rita, had resisted all attempts by other students to include her as a co-actor in the role playing. The trainer was finally able to persuade her to participate in a role play in which Alice was the main actor. As soon as Rita stood up to walk toward the front of the classroom, the teacher decided that social reinforcement was in order, and said: "Rita, I'm glad you decided to help Alice work on Starting a Conversation."

Following the role play, in which Rita gave barely audible responses to Alice's comments, the teacher decided that Rita should be reinforced for her participation (even though her responses were meek, they represented an improvement over her total lack of participation) before providing Alice with feedback on her performance. The trainer looked at Rita and said, "Rita, I'm really pleased that you participated in this role play. Role playing is hard to do, and you did a fine job."

Self-Reinforcement. This refers to the trainee's ability to evaluate his own performance and provide self-rewards for desirable accomplishments. Self-reinforcement is a particularly important form of reward because social and material reinforcements from others in the youngster's environment are not always forthcoming. Typically, self-reinforcement takes the form of tangible self-rewards coupled with positive self-statements. In the context of classroom management, trainees can be taught to gradually assume control over monitoring their own behaviors and providing their own rewards. As the youngster is taught the principles and procedures of self-rewards, the provision of rewards from others, both material and social, can be diminished. Bandura and Perloff (1967) found that self-monitoring of behaviors to be reinforced by elementary school children was as effective in maintaining the prescribed behavior as was reinforcement provided by others.

Meichenbaum (1973) emphasizes the self-instructional aspect of self-reinforcement—what people say to themselves—as an important factor in classroom management. This strategy has been used successfully in teaching the rules or techniques for solving various problems and in evaluating the results of one's efforts. Thus, children have been taught to "talk to themselves" about what they should do and how well they have done.

EXAMPLE
_____

In a Structured Learning class practicing the skill of Negotiating, the instructor suggested that trainees try to reward themselves if they did their homework and used the skill correctly, following all of the skill's steps. Sally came to the next class and reported that she had successfully negotiated with her mother about her babysitting responsibilities for her little sister. Roger reported that although he followed all of the steps, his mother refused to extend his curfew an extra half hour. When asked if he had rewarded himself for doing his best, Roger said that he just went into his room and sulked. The trainer suggested that he give himself a reward for trying, even though the outcome wasn't what he wanted. Roger complained that he had spent his allowance for the week, so that he couldn't possibly afford a reward. The group got involved in helping Roger to select a reward that wouldn't cost anything. After some discussion, Roger decided that his reward would be to go over to a classmate's house one day after school to listen to some records he had especially wanted to hear.

Group Reinforcement. As all trainers who work with adolescents well know, teenagers are very responsive to the influence of their peers. This phenomenon can be utilized to encourage the performance of infrequent but desirable behaviors. In using group reinforcement, the trainer provides a reward (e.g., food, activity, time off) to the entire group contingent upon the cooperative behavior of individual group members. Thus, if the reward is meaningful and desirable to the entire group, group members are likely to put pressure on one another to behave appropriately. This technique may be used to increase desirable but deficient behaviors as well as to decrease excessive, undesirable behaviors. Tsoi and Yule (1976) have demonstrated the effectiveness of this technique in decreasing disruptive classroom behavior. These researchers used extra break time for the entire class as the reinforcer. The provision of rewards to the group as a whole has also been shown by others to be effective in modifying the behaviors of entire groups in the classroom (e.g., Axelrod, 1973; Medland & Stachnik, 1972) and to single individuals in the classroom (Patterson & Anderson, 1964; Walker & Buckley, 1972).

EXAMPLE

Frankie, a boy who had recently come from a residential treatment center into a public school, was often disruptive in the Structured Learning group by monopolizing sessions and making derogatory remarks about other trainees' efforts to role play. Several other trainees had begun to get caught up in Frankie's behavior and were adding insults of their own each time Frankie got started.

In preparing to deal with the problem, the trainer made arrangements to take the entire Structured Learning class on a theater trip at a later date and announced in class that the trip would take place under certain conditions, namely, if trainees began to encourage one another's efforts to participate in class rather than insulting one another for doing so. The trip was a desirable enough group reinforcer that when Frankie began to engage in his usual behavior, the other trainees who had previously acted similarly began instead to demand that Frankie stop disrupting the class.

Shaping. Often a desired behavior, such as volunteering or contributing to a discussion, does not occur with sufficient frequency, accuracy, or complexity in the initial stages of the Structured Learning group. At such times it is useful for the trainer to provide social (or material) reinforcement for successive approximations as the trainee gradually approaches the desired behavior. Thus the trainer can help the unskilled or hesitant youngster work up to the level of proficiency of performance that is desirable for active participation in the group. Sloane (1976) suggests the following rules in shaping social behavior:

> Shaping Rule 1: Find some behavior in which the child is currently engaging that is a better approximation of your goal for him than his usual behavior and reinforce this approximation each time it occurs.

Shaping Rule 2: When an approximation has become more frequent for several days, select a slightly better one for reinforcement and stop reinforcing the first.

Shaping Rule 3: Each approximation should be only slightly different from the last one.

Shaping Rule 4: Let a new approximation receive many reinforcements before moving on to another approximation.

Shaping Rule 5: Never look a gift horse in the mouth, but reinforce any behavior that is better than that currently required. (pp. 68-70)

EXAMPLE

Arthur, an active youngster with a short attention span, frequently engaged in a variety of disruptive activities (fidgeting, stretching, leaving his seat, and wandering around the classroom). His verbal participation in class activities was quite limited and usually irrelevant. The trainer decided that in addition to working on the elimination of disruptive behaviors, his verbal involvement and participation in classroom activities could be shaped. Since Arthur's reading was at grade level, the trainer decided to use this skill as an initial step in shaping increased verbal participation. As a first step, the trainer began to call upon Arthur to read the steps for the skill being taught on the blackboard and reinforce his speaking clearly and audibly. Once this behavior was established the trainer began to shape more spontaneous speech by asking Arthur to comment on the steps as he read them. The trainer could thus be sure that Arthur's attention was focused on relevant material since he had just read the statement he was being asked to comment upon.

Decreasing Undesirable Behaviors

Extinction

Just as reinforcement has been applied primarily toward the goal of increasing behaviors that occur infrequently, its withdrawal can similarly be utilized to decrease the frequency, intensity, or duration of undesired or excessive behaviors. The principle underlying this extinction effect is quite straightforward: behaviors that are not followed by rewards will tend to diminish or decrease. It is sometimes the case that youngsters receive more attention from teachers and peers for undesirable behaviors than they do for prosocial behaviors.

If we appropriately and consistently apply principles of reinforcement and extinction, the prosocial behaviors should be attended to
and reinforced, and the excessive, undesirable behaviors should be
ignored. The study by Hall, Lund, and Jackson (1968) is but one of
several such investigations that have found this principle to be an
effective one in diminishing behaviors such as disputing and talking
out among the youngsters in both regular classes and special education classes.

EXAMPLE

Mike, a 14-year-old in a Structured Learning class at a residential
center, was under considerable stress because of an upcoming court
appearance. The trainer was aware of the problem and noticed that
Mike was showing increased nervousness and agitation in the classroom. He would frequently pace around the back of the room and
hum quietly to himself. In addition to showing some empathy by discussing Mike's court appearance with him and giving him a chance
to role play Preparing for a Difficult Conversation, the trainer decided that Mike's pacing and humming would be likely to extinguish if left alone. Since Mike's behavior was beginning to get a
good deal of attention from peers (giggling, pointing), the trainer felt
it would be useful to instruct the other youngsters in the class on
how to react to Mike. The next class meeting, when Mike began to
pace, the trainer said, ''We all know that Mike has a court date
coming up and that he's feeling kind of tense about it. I think you
could all help Mike the most by leaving him alone right now. When
he wants to rejoin the class, he knows he can.''

Although it may seem contradictory, a youngster's immediate
response to the elimination of positive reinforcement may be a *tem-
porary* increase in just those behaviors the trainer is attempting to
extinguish. This phenomenon is not difficult to understand. Prior
to the trainer's effort to extinguish the behavior, the youngster's
disruptive behaviors were indeed those that succeeded in gaining
attention. When such attention to the behavior is not forthcoming,
the youngster then intensifies her effort to gain reinforcement or
attention through the increased use of the previously reinforced
(now ignored) behavior.

EXAMPLE

Audrey had been gaining a lot of classroom attention by pulling her hair and making sounds during class. It was becoming clear to the trainer that all of the attention served only to increase the unwanted behavior. After instructing the class to ignore Audrey's behavior (as well as instructing Audrey in how she could participate appropriately), the instructor noticed that Audrey's behavior became more, instead of less, disruptive. When the other students complained about the trainer's instructions to ignore the "disgusting sounds," the trainer said, "I know it's hard to ignore what Audrey is doing today. But if we continue to pay attention to what she's doing, she'll just keep on doing it. I think you'll find that when she sees that nobody is going to react anymore, she'll stop making noises and start participating in what we're doing."

Time out is one type of extinction technique that is frequently useful. It involves isolation of the youngster from potential sources of positive reinforcement (e.g., attention from peers) when he is engaging in disruptive behavior and does not respond to other extinction techniques. This procedure should only be employed once youngsters are forewarned as to the specific behaviors which will warrant its use. Most often, the youngster is removed from the training room to some quiet place where stimulation is minimized (e.g., without magazines, other people, or other distractions).

An alternative to actual removal from the class is proposed by Givner and Graubard (1974). These writers suggest that the youngster may be placed in a "time-out condition" while remaining in the classroom. In such an instance, the disruptive youngster is prevented from interacting with others in the classroom by instructing classmates to ignore him. The "time-out condition" is differentiated from simple extinction by the fact that the youngster is removed from *all* sources of reinforcement for a time, while in extinction, reinforcement is withdrawn from a particular behavior.

EXAMPLE

In one Structured Learning group of extremely disruptive and aggressive youngsters, the trainer was beginning to find that classroom disciplining efforts were absorbing most of the group's time. The trainer thus decided to arrange a "time-out condition." The trainer announced, "Starting next week, any group member who actively disrupts the group from accomplishing its goal will be asked to sit outside of the group. The rest of the class is not to talk to the member who has been excluded."

During the next Structured Learning class, Jerry began to disrupt a role play. He took the card containing the skill steps and started to tear it up. The trainer said, "Jerry, if you remember, we made a new class rule last week. Anyone who keeps the class from doing its work will be excluded from the group's activities. I'd like you to sit over on the side of the room for now. When you can cooperate in what we are doing, you can come back and sit with the group."

Punishment

Punishment refers to the use of aversive or negative consequences in an attempt to eliminate or control a problem behavior when it occurs. Research has shown that punishment is not particularly effective for long-term elimination or diminution of problem behaviors but, instead, is typically only useful in the presence of the person administering the punishment. The person who administers the punishment may come to be viewed by the youngster in a negative light. Furthermore, the youngster who has been punished may eventually come to devalue the entire group and may choose to escape in order to avoid the punitive situation. We would advocate the use of extinction techniques or the instructional techniques that will be discussed later in this chapter as preferable to the use of punishment. Extinction or instructional techniques encourage the youngster to be responsible for his own behavior rather than perpetuating the notion of external control of problem behavior. If the trainer chooses punishment techniques, however, several principles should be employed to increase the likelihood of a desired outcome.

1. Group conduct rules should be established and carefully explained so that youngsters have a clear understanding of what constitutes a violation.

2. The possible punitive consequences for rule violation should be specific, realistic, and consistently applied for each violation.

3. As with rewards, the trainer should be sure that the punish-

ment is indeed aversive to the youngster (sometimes what the trainer views negatively may be viewed positively by the youngster) and is applied immediately after the occurrence of the violation.

EXAMPLE

In a Structured Learning class of older adolescents, many with histories of repeated truancy, the trainer began to notice that several of the trainees were coming to class quite late. By prearrangement with the principal, the trainer decided to institute a detention punishment (stay after school twice as long as the amount of class time missed). At the next class meeting, the trainer announced, "In the future, anyone who is late for class by more than five minutes will have to stay after school double the amount of class time missed." When several trainees complained that they had jobs or other activities immediately after school, the trainer knew that he had indeed selected an aversive punishment.

INSTRUCTIONAL TECHNIQUES

This general category of techniques for the management of problem behavior assumes that the youngster who is exhibiting such behavior in the Structured Learning group may be doing so, in part, because of a lack of understanding of performance expectations held by the trainer. Trainers frequently assume that all trainees have an understanding of and are able to perform the often complex tasks expected of them. Trainees with a limited understanding of the task may attempt to cover up their "ignorance" in front of peers by engaging in a variety of disruptive or inappropriate behaviors. Other trainees, in an attempt to avoid being exposed, may withdraw or otherwise disengage from class participation. The previously described reinforcement techniques are of limited usefulness when the desired behavior is not clearly understood by the trainee or not in the youngster's behavioral repertoire. Thus, providing the trainee with specific, concrete, unambiguous instructions as to what is expected prior to requiring the performance of such behaviors will frequently minimize or eliminate many problem behaviors before they start. Re-instruction in desired behaviors will often be useful after problem behaviors appear. There are a number of useful instructional techniques, which we now wish to examine.

Modeling

As described in Chapter 2, this technique involves providing the trainee with good examples of expected behavior. They may be performed by the trainer or by another trainee.

Role Playing

After providing the trainee with an example of appropriate behavior, it is often useful to have the trainee rehearse or role play the desired behavior immediately. Here, modeling and role playing are used to enhance the performance of appropriate in-class behavior rather than as a component of the Structured Learning format for teaching a specific skill. As such, the trainer might model various sorts of classroom participation (e.g., volunteering to role play, providing feedback) prior to asking a trainee to perform these behaviors.

EXAMPLE
<hr>

In a Structured Learning group of rather withdrawn youngsters, the trainer noticed that the trainees were continuing to have a great deal of difficulty in providing useful feedback, despite the fact that the group had been meeting for more than a month. Trainees were making general comments like ''It was OK'' or else not saying anything. The trainer felt that she should model the skill of providing feedback so that discussions might become more productive. Following the next role play of Sharing Something she said, ''I would like to demonstrate the way in which I would like you to give feedback in the future. I would like your comments to be specific and helpful to John, here, who just role played. By helpful, I mean that I would like you to tell him, first, if he followed all of the steps. If he didn't, let him know which ones he missed. If you see any ways he could improve, like speaking up more, or standing differently, or using different words or a different approach, then give him some suggestions about how to do it differently.

''I'll go first and give John some feedback. John, you did a good job in following all of the steps. You did each step and did them in order. The problem you were working on was whether you wanted to take your brother Lonnie to the movies. That meant you would have to share with him the money your grandmother had given you for your birthday. In Step 1 you decided that you would enjoy the movie more if Lonnie went with you, so you decided that you did want to share your birthday money. In Step 2 you were pretty sure that Lonnie would like the idea. In Step 3 you told Lonnie you would like to treat him to a movie with your birthday money. I'll bet there are people in this class who wish they had a brother as generous as you. You spoke loudly and clearly so that you were definitely able to be heard. I think you might work on standing still when you talk. I noticed that you shuffled your feet, and it was a bit distracting.

"Now, I'd like the rest of you to give John some feedback. Would each of you take one step in the skill and tell John how he followed that step. Mary, can you tell John how he did Step 1, what he did correctly and what he could improve upon. . . ."

Providing Structure

A most basic instructional technique, providing structure involves making sure that the trainer's expectations of trainee behavior are made explicit at the outset of training. Rules and regulations, classroom procedures, systems of rewards and punishments, and procedures specific to the Structured Learning class should be carefully explained, thus making the training environment a predictable one. We have indicated earlier that instruction can and should be combined with other behavior management techniques for maximum effectiveness. In this regard, Madsen, Becker, and Thomas (1968) found that the provision of rules governing classroom behavior was effective only when combined with praise for appropriate behavior and the ignoring of inappropriate behavior.

EXAMPLE

A Structured Learning trainer in a class of youngsters exhibiting short attention span found it was useful to explain rules of conduct during the first session. When the youngsters began to behave disruptively (right at the onset of the group), the trainer said, "Before we get started, I want to set up some class rules. This is a group in which we can all have a lot of fun and learn something useful at the same time. In order to get started, though, I'm going to need your full attention so that I can tell you what we're going to do. Once I've finished, you will each get a chance to talk. So the main rule of this group is that everybody listens when someone is talking, when I'm talking, or when one of your classmates is talking. Also, if you don't understand what someone is talking about I hope you will raise your hand and ask whatever question you have.''

Prompting

This refers to simple reinstruction or coaching of trainees during any phase of the Structured Learning group. Prompting can be particularly useful during role playing, since trainees are frequently unsure of how to behave as they try out new skills for the first time. Other trainees, as well as the trainer, can function as coaches during role playing.

EXAMPLE

In a role play of the skill Joining In, Billy was having trouble figuring out what to say when approaching a group of boys starting a baseball game. He reported that he typically just ''hung around,'' waiting to be asked to join in. He told the class that his technique wasn't working and that he would like to try a new approach.

Prior to role playing, the trainer noticed that Billy looked frightened. The trainer decided to have a pre-role play rehearsal in which the class would give Billy suggestions about what to say during the real role play. The trainer said, ''Who can give some suggestions about what Billy can say?'' Bob suggested that Billy say, ''If you guys need another player, I'd like to play.'' Roger said, ''Billy, why don't you just ask 'Can I play?' '' Billy said that he felt afraid to try what was suggested, because he might be turned down. The trainer then said, ''That's really a risk we all take when we want to join in an activity, and I can understand that it feels scary. The other choice, Billy, is to do what you've been doing, and it sounds like you don't like doing that either. Why don't you try role playing the skill using Bob or Roger's suggestion? This isn't a real situation, so it seems like a good place to see how their method works. Then when you have a real joining in situation, you can decide whether you want to use the skill or not. At least you will have had some practice at it.'' At this point, Billy agreed to try the new approach.

Simplification

Some tasks which appear to be uncomplicated to the trainer or more highly skilled trainees may still be too complex for some trainees and thus require further simplification. When the trainer suspects that simplification is needed, he should break the task down into a series of steps (similar to the behavioral steps discussed in Chapter 5) and ask the trainee to do one step at a time. Other types of simplification might involve repetition of instructions in simpler language, fewer instructions at a time, or fewer skill steps role played at one time.

EXAMPLE

In one new Structured Learning group, Annabelle was having difficulty role playing the four steps of Starting a Conversation. She tended to get confused and then just stop talking. The trainer decided to have her go through a role play for each step individually and, after each, she was given feedback and encouragement. When she had completed the four mini–role plays, the trainer then had her put the steps together (two at a time, three at a time, and finally all four steps).

RELATIONSHIP-BASED TECHNIQUES

Psychologists and educators have long known that the better the relationship between the helper and client or trainee, the more positive and productive will be the outcome of their interaction. In fact, some would hold that the establishment and maintenance of a positive relationship is the most potent factor in effecting behavior change in the client. We take the position that a positive relationship between the trainer and trainee in a Structured Learning group is a valuable tool that the trainer should draw on in order to effect desired behavior within the group. Typically, the relationship-based techniques require the trainer to understand broader aspects of the youngster's behavior than might be available through observation in the classroom alone. Thus, the trainer tries to gain some appreciation of the youngster's reasons or motives for behaving in a particular manner and attempts to be responsive to the trainee's needs. There are a number of specific techniques that draw primarily upon the relationship between trainer and trainee. As we have mentioned earlier, these techniques can often be combined with other class-room management techniques for maximum effect.

Empathic Encouragement

Using this technique, the trainer shows the trainee that she under-stands the difficulty the trainee is experiencing and then urges the trainee to participate as instructed. The technique consists of a series of steps designed to accomplish this goal. The steps are as follows.

1. The trainer offers the trainee the opportunity to explain in detail his difficulty in participating as instructed and listens non-defensively.

2. The trainer expresses an understanding of the trainee's be-havior.

3. If appropriate, the trainer responds that the trainee's view is a viable alternative.

4. The trainer restates her view with supporting reasons and probable outcomes.

5. The trainer expresses the appropriateness of delaying a resolu-tion of the problem.

6. The trainer urges the trainee to tentatively try to participate.

EXAMPLE
_____

Rose, a rather temperamental, disruptive trainee, was being particu-larly negative (laughing, mocking) when the trainer was introducing the skill Asking Permission. After trying to ignore her behavior, ex-pecting that it might extinguish, the trainer decided to attempt to discuss Rose's behavior with her in an empathic way. First, the trainer asked Rose to explain her behavior. Rose replied that she thought the skill was ''dumb.'' She said that in her family, if she waited to ask permission for something, she would have to wait for a week. She stated that at home, you just took something if you needed it.

The trainer then said to Rose, ''I can understand how this skill really doesn't work for you at home. Perhaps it's not a skill you would ever want to use at home. However, there are a lot of situa-tions away from home, like here in school, where you really need to ask permission to do certain things, like excusing yourself from the room or getting permission to turn an assignment in late when you've been sick. If you don't get permission and you just go and do these things, you usually wind up in some kind of trouble. Let's hold off on deciding whether or not this is a useful skill until we've had a chance to role play and try it out. Maybe you can try using the skill here in our group, just to see for yourself if it helps get you what you want. OK, Rose?'' Rose agreed to try the skill and was reasonably attentive through most of the session.

Problem Identification

One of the problems often faced by youngsters is that they do not know how to identify the difficulties they are experiencing. In this technique the trainer makes use of his relationship with the trainee and his perception of what is occurring in order to help the youngster identify and categorize the problem behavior. Such categorization or labeling is intended to provide a vehicle for discussion of the problem behavior with the goal of increased understanding so that the behavior can be changed. The trainer's manner of interpreting or labeling may vary according to the situation, as well as according to the relationship between trainer and trainee. At times the trainer may be gentle; at other times she may confront the trainee.

EXAMPLE

Roger had been attending Structured Learning sessions for several weeks, and the trainer observed a pattern starting to emerge in his behavior. After role playing or participating appropriately in other ways early in the group, he would frequently become inattentive and distract the group from its task. Once the pattern was clear to the trainer, she decided to comment upon it to Roger in the hope that some resolution could be reached. She said to Roger, ''Roger, I notice that when the group begins, you are usually ready to participate. After you have had your say, though, it seems that you stop paying attention to what we are doing. I wonder what we can do about that?'' Roger responded by saying that he didn't know what to do in class once he had participated and that frequently he just started thinking about something else. The trainer then decided to use an instructional technique (providing structure) and to tell

Roger about a variety of ways he could participate throughout the class period.

Threat Reduction

In beginning a new undertaking, youngsters may show some signs of fearfulness or anxiety. Since these feelings can result in a variety of disturbing or withdrawing behaviors, it is incumbent upon the trainer to attempt to reduce the threat as quickly as possible. The trainer should seek to create an environment which is supportive of youngsters' efforts to try out new behaviors, even though they may be awkward or otherwise unskilled at the outset. Reassurance, elicitation of group support, even physical contact are all ways of communicating concern and generating a positive atmosphere. The use of the aforementioned instructional techniques, such as simplification and modeling by trainer or trainees, are other useful techniques for reducing threat. Reinforcement of successive approximations of the desired behavior (shaping) as a method of reducing fear or threat in withdrawn children has also been shown to be effective in this regard (Gardner, 1974).

EXAMPLE

In a new Structured Learning class, Cathy was the last to role play. She had declined several invitations from the trainer to get involved and was slumped down in her seat, almost as if to make herself invisible. When the trainer called upon Cathy, she said she couldn't think of anything to role play. The trainer felt that threat reduction by means of offering supportive reassurance would be useful. She called Cathy's name and said, ''Cathy, everyone else has role played, so I guess it's your turn. I know it's not easy to do the first time, but I can almost guarantee that once you get started, you'll find that it's not so bad. Class, maybe we can all think of some situations in which you could use the skill Starting a Conversation so that Cathy can pick a good one to role play.''

Peer Relationship Techniques

As the support of the peer group is so critically important to classroom performance, the trainer should be alert to a variety of methods for managing problem behaviors that capitalize on the use of peer relationships. Some of these techniques have been discussed earlier in this chapter (e.g., group reinforcement, modeling by peers, and threat reduction). As Kazdin (1975) points out, the presence of peers in the trainee's real-life environment provides the advantage of frequent support and encouragement for the performance of target behavior. Recognizing the power of the peer group in influencing behavior, the trainer should seek every opportunity to allow the peer group to manage the behavior. This in no way abrogates the trainer's responsibility to supervise and guide the behavior of all group members. Stram, Cooke, and Apolloni (1976) reviewed the literature on various techniques useful in eliciting the support of peers in modifying classroom behavior and concluded that teacher efforts to modify behavior without peer support are only of limited value. Some peer relationship techniques which can be used, in addition to those considered earlier, are elicitation of peer support and use of peer helpers.

Elicitation of Peer Support

To the extent that the group's goals are valued, peer pressure can be mobilized to support and encourage appropriate behaviors of a particular youngster and discourage or ignore inappropriate behaviors. The trainer's task in this regard becomes one of structuring the group activity so that such support or pressure can be mobilized. The trainer may also elicit specific group support for specific behaviors demonstrated by hesitant or less skilled group members.

EXAMPLE

The trainer had noticed an increase in frequency of negative comments, insults, and jokes in the class during and after role playing. It was clear that trainees were not being supportive of one another's efforts to learn new skills. In trying to deal with the problem, the trainer decided to teach the skill Giving a Compliment. He made the role play task one of giving a true compliment to someone in the class about how they were doing in class. Trainees had to think a while, but were eventually able to compliment one another about helpfulness, speaking up better, etc. When the next skill was taught, the trainer gave the class the task of giving a compliment to each trainee who had role played (during the feedback part of the group).

Helper Principle

Research has demonstrated consistently that the youngster who is given the task of teaching, helping, or tutoring a peer will be more greatly involved in the task and will be more likely to master the skill or subject matter being taught than youngsters who are not placed in the helper role. Litwak (1977) found this principle operated with adolescents learning a skill in a Structured Learning group. The helper technique may be particularly useful for the youngster who frequently exhibits disruptive behaviors rather than focusing on the task of the group, thus channeling his attention into the task-related aspects of the Structured Learning group.

EXAMPLE

One Structured Learning trainer decided to employ the helper principle with Heather, a youngster who spent a good deal of time "clowning around" during role play in an apparent effort to cover up her embarrassment at performing. The trainer asked Heather to stay after class and invited her to serve as "teacher aide" during the next class, when the skill of Expressing Your Feelings was to be taught. The trainer explained that as an aide, Heather would do live modeling with the trainer in order to demonstrate to the class how to use the skill correctly. To prepare for this, Heather and the trainer would get together before class and rehearse several modeling skits. Following the rehearsal session and discussion with Heather about the importance of modeling the skill accurately, Heather was able to do a competent job of modeling.

The trainer noticed that during that class Heather was more active than in other sessions in giving feedback when others role played. Also, when called upon to role play a situation from her own life, she seemed to take the challenge more seriously.

SUMMARY

Problematic behaviors occurring in a Structured Learning group are viewed as those behaviors that interfere with or detract from the task-oriented, ongoing nature of the group. We have categorized them broadly as excessive behaviors and deficient behaviors and have described a variety of techniques for dealing with specific types of excesses or deficiencies. Behavior modification techniques, instructional techniques, and relationship-based techniques have been described. All of these techniques share the common goal of helping the youngster to become actively involved in the Structured Learning group so that the skills being taught can be learned and practiced. We feel that it is the trainer's responsibility to identify problem behavior as soon as possible and select and apply one or more relevant remediation or management techniques.

CHAPTER 8

Structured Learning Research:
An Annotated Bibliography

Training and treatment approaches that aspire to assist people in leading more effective and more satisfying lives must not be permitted to endure indefinitely simply on the basis of the faith and enthusiasm of their proponents. Whether psychoeducational or of other types, such interventions must be subjected to careful, objective, and continuing evaluation. Only those approaches that research demonstrates to be effective deserve society's continued use and development. Those that fail such evaluations justly must not be used.

The present chapter reports, in annotated bibliographic form, a number of completed and ongoing evaluative studies examining the effectiveness of Structured Learning, as well as a small number of other reports dealing with particular aspects or implications of this approach. The references to several studies involving adolescent and pre-adolescent trainees receiving Structured Learning in schools, residential centers, or correctional settings are printed in boldface. Structured Learning is abbreviated as SL; Structured Learning Therapy is SLT.

In general terms, the several evaluative studies reported here combine to support the effectiveness of Structured Learning with diverse trainee groups and diverse skill-training targets. Much remains to be learned about this training approach, and continuing tests of its efficacy are necessary. But, on the basis of evidence described below, we are confident in recommending its continued and expanded use with adolescent and adult trainees.

Berlin, R. J. *Training of hospital staff in accurate affective perception of fear-anxiety from vocal cues in the context of varying facial cues.* Unpublished masters thesis, Syracuse University, 1974.
Trainees: Attendants and nurses (N = 52)
Skill: Recognition of vocal cues of anxiety
Experimental design: (1) SL for vocal and facial cues, (2) SL for vocal cues, (3) No-training control
Results: No significant between-group differences. For group receiving SL for both vocal and facial cues, a significant pre-post recognition gain on both training and test cues of anxiety.

————. *Teaching acting-out adolescents prosocial conflict resolution with Structured Learning Therapy.* Unpublished doctoral dissertation, Syracuse University, 1977.
Trainees: Adolescent boys with history of acting-out behaviors (N = 42)
Skill: Empathy
Experimental design: (1) SL for empathy in conflict situations, (2) SL for empathy in nonconflict situations, versus (3) No-treatment control by (a) High Interpersonal Maturity Level versus (b) Low Interpersonal Maturity Level
Results: SL for empathy (conflict) significantly > SL for empathy (nonconflict) or controls on acquisition. High I level significantly > Low I level. No significant generalization effects.

Bleeker, D. J. *Structured Learning Therapy with skill-deficient adolescents.* Unpublished masters thesis, Syracuse University, in progress.
Trainees: Adolescent boys identified as disruptive in regular junior high school (N = 55)
Skill: Responding to a complaint
Experimental design: A 2 × 2 plus control factorial design reflecting high versus low perceived (by the trainee) similarity between SL trainer and generalization test figure by high versus low objective similarity, plus brief instructions control
Results: In progress.

Cobb, F. M. *Acquisition and retention of cooperative behavior in young boys through instructions, modeling, and structured learning.* Unpublished doctoral dissertation, Syracuse University, 1973.
Trainees: First-grade boys (N = 80)
Skill: Cooperation
Experimental design: (1) SL for cooperation, (2) Instructions plus modeling of cooperation, (3) Instructions for cooperation, (4) Attention control, (5) No-treatment control
Results: SL significantly > all other conditions on both immediate and delayed tests of cooperative behavior.

Cross, W. *An investigation of the effects of therapist motivational predispositions in Structured Learning Therapy under task versus relationship stress conditions.* Unpublished doctoral dissertation, Syracuse University, 1977.
Trainees: College undergraduates (N = 120)
Skill: Structured Learning Therapy group leadership skills
Experimental design: Task-motivated versus relationship-motivated trainers by task-relevant versus relationship-relevant trainee-originated trainer stress plus no-treatment control
Results: Relationship-motivated trainers significantly > task-motivated trainers on SL effectiveness under task threat conditions.

Davis, C. *Training police in crisis intervention skills.* Unpublished manuscript, Syracuse University, September 1974.
Description of a training program utilizing SL to develop skills among a 225-person urban police force for the competent handling of family fights, rapes, accidents, suicides, and variety of other crises common in everyday police work. Skills taught included: 1) Preparing to deal with threats to your safety; 2) Calming the emotional aspects of the crisis; 3) Gathering relevant information; and 4) Taking appropriate action.

Edelman, E. *Behavior of high versus low hostility – guilt Structured Learning trainers under standardized client conditions of expressed hostility.* Unpublished masters thesis, Syracuse University, 1977.
Trainers: Nurses and attendants at state mental hospital (N = 60)
Skill: Structured learning trainer group leadership behaviors
Experimental design: SL trainers high versus low in hostility-guilt by (1) High, (2) Low or (3) No expressed client hostility
Results: High hostility-guilt trainers respond to trainee hostility with significantly less counterhostility than do Low hostility-guilt trainers. Low hostility-guilt trainers significantly > counterhostility to hostile than neutral trainees; no similar effect for High hostility-guilt trainers.

———. *Effect of helper communication of high versus low empathy and genuineness on delinquent adolescents' attraction and approach behavior to helper.* Unpublished doctoral dissertation, Syracuse University, in progress.
Trainees: Adolescent boys at I levels 3, 4, and 5, residing in centers for adjudicated juvenile delinquents (N = 90)
Experimental design: A 3 × 3 factorial with three I levels of adolescent interviewees compared against three levels of interviewer empathy and genuineness on in-interview speech behavior and post-interview relationship criteria
Results: In progress.

Figueroa-Torres, J. *Structured Learning Therapy: Its effects upon self-control of aggressive fathers from Puerto Rican low socioeconomic families.*

Unpublished doctoral dissertation, Syracuse University, 1978.
Trainees: Family abusing fathers (N = 60)
Skill: Self-control
Experimental design: SL for self-control versus no-treatment
Results: SL-trained fathers significantly > controls on self-control on acquisition and minimal generalization criteria.

Fleming, D. *Teaching negotiation skills to preadolescents.* Unpublished doctoral dissertation, Syracuse University, 1977.
Trainees: Adolescents (N = 96)
Skill: Negotiation
Experimental design: High self-esteem versus Low self-esteem adolescents by Adult SL trainer versus Peer SL trainer by Presence versus Absence of pre-SL enhancement of expectancy for success
Results: All SL groups showed significant increase in negotiation skill acquisition but not transfer. No significant effects between trainer type or between esteem level effects.

Fleming, L. R. *Training aggressive and unassertive educable mentally retarded children for assertive behaviors, using three types of Structured Learning Therapy.* Unpublished doctoral dissertation, Syracuse University, 1977.
Trainees: Mentally retarded children (N = 96)
Skill: Assertiveness
Experimental design: (1) SL for assertiveness plus fear-coping training, (2) SL for assertiveness plus anger-coping training, (3) SL for assertiveness, (4) Attention control by Aggressive versus Unassertive children
Results: All three SL groups significantly > controls on increase in assertiveness. No significant *in vivo* transfer effects.

Friedenberg, W. P. *Verbal and nonverbal attraction modeling in an initial therapy interview analogue.* Unpublished masters thesis, Syracuse University, 1971.
Trainees: Psychiatric inpatients (N = 60, all male, mostly schizophrenic)
Skill: Attraction
Experimental design: High versus low attraction to interviewer displayed via nonverbal cues by high versus low attraction to interviewer displayed via verbal cues
Results: Significant modeling effect for attraction for the High-High group (high modeled attraction using both the verbal and nonverbal cues) as compared to the other three conditions.

Gilstad, R. *Acquisition and transfer of empathic responses by teachers through self-administered and leader-directed Structured Learning Training and the interaction between training method and conceptual level.* Unpublished doctoral dissertation, Syracuse University, 1977.
Trainees: Elementary school teachers (N = 60)
Skill: Empathy

Experimental design: SL for empathy, training conducted by a trainer in "standard" SL groups versus SL for empathy, self-instructional training format by High versus Low conceptual level trainees, plus attention control
Results: Both SL groups significantly > control on empathy, on acquisition, and transfer criteria. No significant effects between SL conditions or between conceptual levels.

Golden, R. *Teaching resistance-reducing behavior to high school students.* Unpublished doctoral dissertation, Syracuse University, 1975.
Trainees: High school students (N = 43)
Skill: Resistance-reducing behavior (reflection of the other's feeling plus appropriate assertiveness regarding one's own view in an interpersonal conflict situation with authority figures)
Experimental design: (1) Discrimination training ("good" modeled skill behavior versus "bad" modeled skill behavior) for resistance-reducing behavior, (2) SL for resistance-reducing behavior, (3) No-treatment control by Internal versus External locus of control
Results: Both Discrimination Training and SL significantly > controls on resistance-reducing behavior on both acquisition and generalization criteria. No significant locus of control effects.

Goldstein, A. P. A prescriptive psychotherapy for the alcoholic patient based on social class. In *Proceedings of the Second Annual Alcoholism Conference of NIAAA.* Washington, D.C.: U.S. Department of Health, Education and Welfare, 1973, pp. 234-241.
An overview of the development of Structured Learning Therapy and relevant evaluative research, with special emphasis upon its implications for alcoholic patients.

———. *Structured Learning Therapy: Toward a psychotherapy for the poor.* New York: Academic Press, 1974.
A comprehensive statement of the origin and rationale for Structured Learning Therapy and a full presentation of relevant evaluative research. Modeling scripts from both inpatient and outpatient studies are presented.
Contents: 1) Psychotherapy: Income and outcome; 2) Personality development and preparation for patienthood; 3) Language and malcommunication; 4) Psychopathology and sociopathology; 5) Structured Learning and the middle-class patient; 6) Structured Learning and the lower-class inpatient; 7) Structured Learning and the lower-class outpatient; 8) Structured Learning and the working-class paraprofessional; 9) Future directions; Appendix: Modeling scripts

Goldstein, A. P., Cohen, R., Blake, G., & Walsh, W. The effects of modeling and social class structuring in paraprofessional psychotherapist train-

ing. *Journal of Nervous and Mental Diseases,* 1971, *153,* 47-56.
Trainees: Nurses and attendants (N = 135)
Skill: Attraction, empathy, warmth
Experimental design: High, low, and no attraction modeling by middle, low, and no social class structuring
Results: Significant modeling by social class–structuring interaction effects for attraction, empathy, and warmth.

Goldstein, A. P., & Goedhart, A. W. The use of Structured Learning for empathy enhancement in paraprofessional psychotherapist training. *Journal of Community Psychology,* 1973, *1,* 168-173.
Experiment I.
Trainees: Student nurses (N = 74)
Skill: Empathy
Experimental design: (1) SL for empathy (professional trainers), (2) SL for empathy (paraprofessional trainers), (3) No-training control
Results: Both SL conditions significantly > No-training control on both immediate and generalization measures of empathy.
Experiment II.
Trainees: Hospital staff (N = 90, nurses, attendants, occupational therapists, recreational therapists)
Skill: Empathy
Experimental design: (1) SL plus transfer training for empathy, (2) SL for empathy, (3) No-training control
Results: Significant SL effect for immediate empathy measurement (Groups 1 and 2 > 3); significant transfer effect for generalization empathy measure (Group 1 > 2 and 3).

Goldstein, A. P., Goedhart, A. W., & Wijngaarden, H. R. Modeling in de psychotherapie bij patienten uit de lagere sociale klasse. In A. P. Cassee, P. E. Boeke, & J. T. Barendregt (Eds.), *Klinische Psychologie in Nederland.* Deventer: Van Loghum Slaterus, 1973, pp. 279-288.

A presentation (in Dutch) of the origin, rationale, and current status of Structured Learning Therapy. The particular usefulness of this approach with low-income Dutch and American patient populations is stressed.

Goldstein, A. P., Hoyer, W., & Monti, P. J. (Eds.). *Police and the elderly.* New York: Pergamon Press, 1979.

The special needs and problems of elderly citizens, as these relate to the role of police, is the primary focus of this book. Means by which police, other criminal justice personnel, and the elderly themselves can assist in preventing crime against the elderly and minimizing its psychological import when it does occur are among the topics addressed. Use of Structured Learning to train police in these roles is systematically presented.
Contents: 1) The elderly: Who are they?; 2) Fear of crime and the elderly; 3) Minority elderly; 4) Crime prevention with elderly citizens; 5) Police investigation with elderly citizens; 6) Assisting the elderly victim;

7) Training the elderly in mastery of the environment; 8) Training police for work with the elderly

Goldstein, A. P., Martens, J., Hubben, J., Van Belle, H., Schaaf, W., Wiersema, H., & Goedhart, A. The use of modeling to increase independent behavior. *Behavior Research and Therapy*, 1973, *11*, 31-42.
Experiment I.
Trainees: Psychiatric outpatients (N = 90, all psychoneurotic or character disorders)
Skill: Independence (assertiveness)
Experimental design: (1) Independence modeling, (2) Dependence modeling, (3) No-modeling
Results: Significant modeling effect for Independence and a significant modeling effect for Dependence, both as compared to each other and to the No-modeling control condition.
Experiment II.
Trainees: Psychiatric outpatients (N = 60, all psychoneurotic or character disorders)
Skill: Independence (assertiveness)
Experimental design: Independence modeling plus (1) Structuring model as warm, (2) Structuring model as cold, (3) No structuring of model by Male versus Female plus a No-structuring/No-modeling control
Results: Warm and no-structuring modeling conditions significantly > cold structuring and control on independence for males and females.
Experiment III.
Trainees: Psychiatric inpatients (N = 54, all schizophrenic)
Skill: Independence (assertiveness)
Experimental design: Presence versus Absence of independence modeling by Presence versus Absence of instructions to behave independently
Results: Significant main and interaction effects for modeling and instructions on independence as compared to no-modeling/no-instructions conditions.

Goldstein, A. P., Monti, P. J., Sardino, T. J., & Green, D. J. *Police crisis intervention.* New York: Pergamon Press, 1977.
   An applied text oriented toward law enforcement and criminal justice personnel concerned with effective handling of diverse order maintenance and police service matters.
Contents: 1) Introduction; 2) Crisis intervention manual for police; 3) Family disputes; 4) Mental disturbance; 5) Drug and alcohol intoxication; 6) Rape; 7) Suicide; 8) A method for effective training: Structured Learning; 9) Structured Learning manual for police trainers

Goldstein, A. P., Sherman, M., Gershaw, N. J., Sprafkin, R. P., & Glick, B. Training aggressive adolescents in prosocial behavior. *Journal of Youth and Adolescence,* 1978, *7,* 73-92.
   A comprehensive review of research employing SL with aggressive

adolescent trainees. Study designs and findings are presented and examined. The value of prescriptively designed practice and research is emphasized. Special emphasis is placed upon transfer of training, particularly reasons for its infrequency, and possible means for its enhancement.

Goldstein, A. P., & Sorcher, M. Changing managerial behavior by applied learning techniques. *Training and Development Journal,* March 1973, 36-39.

An examination of inadequacies characterizing most managerial training approaches, including 1) the singular focus on attitude change rather than behavior change; 2) unresponsiveness to changing characteristics of the American work force; and 3) insufficient attention to the implications of research on human learning for managerial training. The manner in which Structured Learning seeks to correct these inadequacies and provide an effective approach to training managers is presented.

———. *Changing supervisor behavior.* New York: Pergamon Press, 1974.

An applied presentation of Structured Learning, oriented toward the teaching of supervisory skills, especially in industry. Relevant evaluative research in an industrial context is reported.

Contents: 1) Supervisor training: Perspectives and problems; 2) A focus on behavior; 3) Modeling; 4) Role playing; 5) Social reinforcement; 6) Transfer training; 7) Applied learning; Applications and evidence

Goldstein, A. P., Sprafkin, R. P., & Gershaw, N. J. Structured Learning Therapy: Skill training for schizophrenics. *Schizophrenia Bulletin,* 1975, *14,* 83-88.

A description of the procedures that constitute Structured Learning Therapy and their evaluation. Relevant modeling tapes and related materials are also described. This article places special emphasis on the community-relevant needs of a variety of types of schizophrenic patients and the manner in which daily living skill deficits may be systematically reduced by the use of this approach.

———. *Skill training for community living: Applying Structured Learning Therapy.* New York: Pergamon Press, 1976.

A detailed, applied presentation regarding the use of Structured Learning Therapy with adult psychiatric patients and similar trainees.

Contents: 1) Introduction; 2) Trainer preparation and training procedures; 3) Inpatient and outpatient trainees; 4) Modeling tapes; 5) SLT research; Supplement A. Trainer's Manual; Supplement B. Trainee's Notebook; Supplement C. An advanced SLT session; Supplement D. Resistance and resistance reduction; Supplement E. Skill surveys

———. *I know what's wrong, but I don't know what to do about it.* Englewood Cliffs, N.J.: Prentice-Hall, 1979.

A self-administered version of Structured Learning, presented in stepwise, concrete detail. Oriented in content and procedures toward the general, adult population.

Contents: 1) How to use this book; 2) Knowing what's wrong: Diagnosing the problem; 3) Getting ready: Preparing to change your behavior; 4) What to do about it: Changing your behavior; 5) Personal skills in action: Guidelines, steps and examples; 6) Making changes stick; 7) More personal skills

Greenleaf, D. *The use of programmed transfer of training and Structured Learning Therapy with disruptive adolescents in a school setting.* Unpublished masters thesis, Syracuse University, 1978.
Trainees: Adolescent boys with history of disruptive behavior (N = 43)
Skill: Helping others
Experimental design: SL versus No SL by Transfer Programming versus No Transfer Programming plus Attention Control
Results: SL showed significantly greater skill acquisition, minimal generalization, and extended generalization than either No SL or Attention Control. Transfer Programming did not augment this significant transfer effect.

Gutride, M. E., Goldstein, A. P., & Hunter, G. F. The use of modeling and role playing to increase social interaction among schizophrenic patients. *Journal of Consulting and Clinical Psychology,* 1973, *40,* 408-415.
Trainees: Psychiatric inpatients (N = 133, all "asocial, withdrawn")
Skill: Social interaction (an array of conversational and physical approach skill behaviors)
Experimental design: SL versus No SL by Psychotherapy versus No Psychotherapy by Acute versus Chronic
Result: A substantial number of significant interaction and main effects for SL across several social interaction behavioral criteria.

Gutride, M. E., Goldstein, A. P., & Hunter, G. F. Structured Learning Therapy with transfer training for chronic inpatients. *Journal of Clinical Psychology,* July 1974, *30,* 277-280.
Trainees: Psychiatric inpatients (N = 106, all "asocial, withdrawn")
Skill: Social interaction in a mealtime context
Experimental design: (1) SL plus transfer training, (2) SL plus additional SL, (3) SL, (4) Companionship control, (5) No-treatment control
Results: A substantial number of significant effects for SL across several social interaction behavioral criteria. Significant effects are mainly for groups 1, 2, and 3 compared to the control conditions, rather than between the SL conditions.

Guzzetta, R. A. *Acquisition and transfer of empathy by the parents of early adolescents through Structured Learning Training.* Unpublished doctoral dissertation, Syracuse University, 1974.
Trainees: Mothers of early adolescents (N = 37)

Skill: Empathy
Experimental design: (1) SL for empathy taught to mothers and their children together (to maximize transfer), (2) SL for empathy taught to mothers and their children separately, (3) SL for empathy taught to mothers only, (4) No-training control
Results: All three SL conditions showed significantly greater acquisition and transfer of empathy than did No-training control mothers. No significant differences between SL conditions.

Healy, J. A. *Training of hospital staff in accurate effective perception of anger from vocal cues in the context of varying, facial cues.* Unpublished masters thesis, Syracuse University, 1975.
Trainees: Nurses and attendants (N = 44)
Skill: Recognition of vocal cues of anger
Experimental design: (1) SL for vocal and facial cues, (2) SL for vocal cues with exposure to but no training for facial cues, (3) SL for vocal cues, (4) No-training control
Results: All SL groups significantly > controls on vocal training and test cues; no significant generalization to new (untrained) vocal cues.

Healy, J. A. **Structured Learning therapy and the promotion of transfer of training through the employment of overlearning and stimulus variability.** Unpublished doctoral dissertation, Syracuse University, in progress.
Trainees: Unassertive adolescents in regular junior high school (N = 84)
Skill: Assertiveness
Experimental design: A 3 × 2 plus control factorial design reflecting the presence versus absence of stimulus variability by three levels of overlearning, plus brief instructions control
Results: In progress.

Hollander, T. G. *The effects of role playing on attraction, disclosure, and attitude change in a psychotherapy analogue.* Unpublished doctoral dissertation, Syracuse University, 1970.
Trainees: V. A. hospital psychiatric inpatients (N = 45, all males)
Skill: Attraction to the psychotherapist
Experimental design: Role play versus Exposure versus No-treatment control
Results: No significant role-playing effects for attraction or disclosure.

Hummel, J. **Session variability and skill content as transfer enhancers in Structured Learning training.** Unpublished doctoral dissertation, Syracuse University, 1979.
Trainees: Aggressive pre-adolescents (N = 47)
Skill: Self-control, Negotiation
Experimental design: SL-variable conditions versus SL-constant conditions by self-control skill versus negotiation skill versus both

Results: SL-variable conditions significantly > SL-constant conditions on both acquisition and transfer dependent measures across both skills singly and combined.

Jennings, R. L. *The use of Structured Learning techniques to teach attraction-enhancing interviewee skills to residentially hospitalized, lower socioeconomic emotionally disturbed children and adolescents: A psychotherapy analogue investigation.* Unpublished doctoral dissertation, University of Iowa, 1975.
Trainees: Emotionally disturbed, lower socioeconomic children and adolescents (N = 40)
Skill: Interviewee behaviors: initiation, terminating silences, elaboration, and expression of affect.
Experimental design: (1) SL for interviewee behaviors versus (2) Minimal treatment control in a 2 × 2 × 4 factorial design reflecting (a) repeated measures, (b) treatments, and (c) interviewers
Results: SL significantly > Minimal treatment control on interview initiation and terminating silences. No significant effects on interview elaboration or expression of affect. SL significantly > Minimal treatment control on attractiveness to interviewer on portion of study measures.

Lack, D. Z. *The effect of a model and instructions on psychotherapist self-disclosure.* Unpublished masters thesis, Syracuse University, 1971.
Trainees: Attendants (N = 60)
Skill: Self-disclosure
Experimental design: Presence versus Absence of modeled self-disclosure by Presence versus Absence of instructions to self-disclose
Results: Significant modeling and instruction effects for self-disclosure.

————. *Problem-solving training, Structured Learning training, and didactic instruction in the preparation of paraprofessional mental health personnel for the utilization of contingency management techniques.* Unpublished doctoral dissertation, Syracuse University, 1975.
Trainees: Nurses and attendants (N = 50)
Skill: Contingency management
Experimental design: SL for problem solving and contingency management versus SL for contingency management by Instruction for problem solving and contingency management versus Instruction for contingency management plus No-training control
Results: Significant SL effects for problem solving.

Liberman, B. *The effect of modeling procedures on attraction and disclosure in a psychotherapy analogue.* Unpublished doctoral dissertation, Syracuse University, 1970.
Trainees: Alcoholic inpatients (N = 84, all males)
Skill: Self-disclosure; attraction to the psychotherapist
Experimental design: High versus Low modeled self-disclosure by High

versus Low modeled attraction plus Neutral-tape and No-tape controls
Results: Significant modeling effect for self-disclosure; no modeling effect for attraction.

Litwak, S. E. *The use of the helper therapy principle to increase therapeutic effectiveness and reduce therapeutic resistance: Structured Learning Therapy with resistant adolescents.* Unpublished doctoral dissertation, Syracuse University, 1977.
Trainees: Junior high school students (N = 48)
Skill: Following instructions
Experimental design: (1) SL for following instructions, trainees anticipate serving as SL trainers, (2) SL for following instructions, no trainee anticipation of serving as trainers, versus (3) No-treatment control by three parallel conditions involving Expressing a Compliment, i.e., a skill target not concerned with resistance reduction
Results: Group 1 significantly > Group 2 significantly > Group 3 on both skills on immediate posttest and transfer measures.

Lopez, M. A. *The influence of vocal and facial cue training on the identification of affect communicated via paralinguistic cues.* Unpublished masters thesis, Syracuse University, 1974.
Trainees: Nurses and attendants (N = 52)
Skill: Recognition of vocal cues of depression
Experimental design: (1) SL for vocal and facial cues, (2) SL, (3) SL for vocal cues, (4) No-training control.
Results: SL for vocal cues plus either facial cue training (Group 1) or facial cue exposure (Group 2) significantly > SL for vocal cues (Group 3) or No-training control (Group 4) on post-test and generalization criteria.

Lopez, M., Hoyer, W., & Goldstein, A. P. *Effects of overlearning and incentive on the acquisition and transfer of interpersonal skills with institutionalized elderly patients.* Unpublished manuscript, Syracuse University, 1979.
Trainees: Elderly inpatients in state hospital (N = 56)
Skill: Starting a conversation
Experimental design: SL plus high versus moderate versus low overlearning by presence versus absence of material reinforcement
Results: Significant skill acquisition effect across SL conditions; significant transfer-enhancement effect for both overlearning and concrete reinforcement.

Miron, M., & Goldstein, A. P. *Hostage.* New York: Pergamon Press, 1978.
    An applied presentation oriented toward law enforcement and criminal justice personnel concerned with hostage and terrorism situations.
Contents: 1) Introduction; 2) The Cotton case; 3) The Kiritsis case; 4) The Hanafi Muslim case; 5) The Hearst case; 6) The media,

"shrinks" and other civilians; 7) Hostage negotiation procedures; 8) A method for effective training: Structured Learning; 9) Structured Learning manual for police trainers

Moses, J. *Supervisory relationship training: A new approach to supervisory training, results of evaluation research.* New York: Human Resources Development Department, AT&T, May 1974.
Trainees: Supervisor trainees (N = 183)
Skill: Effective management of an array of supervisor-supervisee relationship problems involving discrimination, absenteeism, and theft
Experimental design: SL for supervisory relationship skills versus No training
Results: Trained supervisors significantly > untrained supervisors on all behavioral and questionnaire criteria.

O'Brien, D. *Trainer-trainee FIRO-B compatibility as a determinant of certain process events in Structured Learning Therapy.* Unpublished masters thesis, Syracuse University, 1977.
Trainees: Nurses and attendants at state mental hospital (N = 60)
Skill: Structured Learning trainer group leadership behaviors vis à vis low affection (actor) trainees
Experimental design: Trainers with High versus Low Originator Compatability for FIRO-B Control by Compatible or Incompatible trainees; also, trainers with High versus Low Originator Compatibility for FIRO-B Affection by Compatible or Incompatible trainees.
Results: No significant between-trainer effects. No significant trainer by trainee effects. Trainers more competent but less warm with cold, versus neutral, trainees.

Orenstein, R. *The influence of self-esteem on modeling behavior in a psychotherapy analogue.* Unpublished masters thesis, Syracuse University, 1969.
Trainees: University undergraduates (N = 80, all females)
Skill: Attraction to the psychotherapist
Experimental design: High versus Low modeled attraction by High versus Low subject self-esteem
Results: Significant modeling effect for attraction; no modeling effect for self-esteem. Subjects viewing a high attraction model were also significantly more willing to disclose, as were high self-esteem subjects. Low self-esteem subjects were significantly more persuasible.

Orenstein, R. *Effect of training patients to focus on their feelings on level of experiencing in a subsequent interview.* Unpublished doctoral dissertation, Syracuse University, 1973.
Trainees: Psychiatric inpatients (N = 75, all female)
Skill: Focusing (ability to be aware of one's own affective experiencing)
Experimental design: (1) SL for focusing, (2) Focusing manual, (3) Brief

instruction for focusing, (4) Attention control, (5) No-treatment control
Results: No significant between-group differences in focusing ability.

Perry, M. A. *Didactic instructions for and modeling of empathy.* Unpublished doctoral dissertation, Syracuse University, 1970.
Trainees: Clergymen (N = 66)
Skill: Empathy
Experimental design: High empathy modeling versus Low empathy modeling versus No modeling by Presence versus Absence of instructions to be empathic
Results: Significant modeling effect for empathy. No significant instructions or interaction effects for empathy.

Perry, M. A. **Structured Learning Therapy for skill training of mentally retarded children.** Unpublished manuscript, University of Washington, 1976.
Trainees: Mildly and moderately retarded halfway house residents (N = 36)
Skill: Social interaction skills
Experimental design: SL for social interaction skills versus Attention control versus No-treatment control
Results: SL significantly > controls on mealtime social interaction skills.

Raleigh, R. **Individual versus group Structured Learning Therapy for assertiveness training with senior and junior high school students.** Unpublished doctoral dissertation, Syracuse University, 1977.
Trainees: Senior and junior high school students (N = 80)
Skill: Assertiveness
Experimental design: Individual versus group SL by senior versus junior high school student trainees plus attention control and no-treatment control
Results: SL in groups significantly > all other SL and control conditions on assertiveness on both acquisition and transfer criteria.

Robertson, B. *The effects of Structured Learning trainer's need to control on their group leadership behavior with aggressive and withdrawn trainees.* Unpublished masters thesis, Syracuse University, 1978.
Trainers: Nurses and attendants at state mental hospital (N = 60)
Skill: Structured learning trainer group leadership behaviors
Experimental design: Trainers high or low on need to control in interpersonal contexts versus controlling or cooperative actor trainees
Results: Trainers high on need to control significantly > competence with actively resistant trainees than trainers low on need to control. High need to control trainers significantly > attraction to actively resistive than neutral trainees.

Robinson, R. *Evaluation of a Structured Learning empathy training program for lower socioeconomic status home-aide trainees.* Unpublished masters thesis, Syracuse University, 1973.
Trainees: Home-aide trainees (N = 29)
Skill: Empathy
Experimental design: (1) SL for empathy, (2) Didactic training of empathy, (3) No-treatment control
Results: SL > Didactic training or No-treatment control on immediate posttest and generalization measures of empathy.

Rosenthal, N. *Matching counselor trainees' conceptual level and training approaches: A study in the acquisition and enhancement of confrontation skills.* Unpublished doctoral dissertation, Syracuse University, 1975.
Trainees: Counselor trainees (N = 60)
Skill: Confrontation (ability to point out to clients discrepancies in the verbal and/or nonverbal contents of their statements)
Experimental design: SL for confrontation, training conducted by a trainer in ''standard'' SL groups versus SL for confrontation, self-instructional training format, by High versus Low conceptual level trainees, plus Attention Control
Results: Significant interaction effects on confrontation skill for type of SL (leader-led versus self-instructional) by conceptual level (high versus low). SL (both types) > Attention Control on confrontation skill.

Schneiman, R. *An evaluation of Structured Learning and didactic learning as methods of training behavior modification skills to lower and middle socioeconomic level teacher-aides.* Unpublished doctoral dissertation, Syracuse University, 1972.
Trainees: Teacher aides (N = 60, 30 middle-class and 30 lower-class)
Skill: Disciplining (appropriate use of rules, disapproval, and praise)
Experimental design: (1) SL for disciplining, (2) Didactic training for disciplining, (3) No-training control by Middle-class versus Lower-class aides
Results: Across social-class levels, SL > Didactic or No-training on immediate and generalization behavioral measures of disciplining.

Shaw, L. W. *A study of empathy training effectiveness: Comparing computer assisted instruction, Structured Learning training and encounter training exercises.* Unpublished doctoral dissertation, Syracuse University, 1978.
Trainees: College undergraduates (N = 93)
Skill: Empathy
Experimental design: Computer assisted instruction versus SL versus encounter training versus No training control for empathy
Results: Computer assisted instruction and SL significantly > No-training control on level of empathy.

Solomon, E. J. *Structured Learning Therapy with abusive parents: Training in self-control.* Unpublished doctoral dissertation, Syracuse University, 1978.
Trainees: Child abusing parents (N = 40, 31 female and 9 male)
Skill: Self-control
Experimental design: SL with and without structuring into helper role by SL with and without mastery training plus brief instructions control
Results: All SL groups significantly > controls on self-control on both acquisition and generalization criteria. SL plus helper structuring plus mastery training significantly > all other SL groups.

Sorcher, M., & Goldstein, A. P. A behavior modeling approach in training. *Personnel Administration,* 1973, *35,* 35-41.
An overview on the nature and potential impact of Structured Learning in an industrial context. Topics examined include the need for a concrete, behavioral training focus; the basis for the choice of modeling, role playing, social reinforcement, and transfer training as the desirable components of this behavioral approach; and a brief example of how these procedures are utilized.

Sprafkin, R. P., Gershaw, N. J., & Goldstein, A. P. Teaching interpersonal skills to psychiatric outpatients: Using Structured Learning Therapy in a community-based setting. *Journal of Rehabilitation,* 1978, *44,* 26-29.
A presentation of the rationale, procedures, and materials of Structured Learning Therapy. Its potential rehabilitative usefulness in fostering effective and satisfying community functioning is stressed.

Sturm, D. *Therapist aggression tolerance and dependency tolerance under standardized client conditions of hostility and dependency.* Unpublished masters thesis, Syracuse University, in progress.
Trainees: Parent aides employed at child abuse agency (N = 28)
Skill: Structured Learning leadership skills
Experimental design: Two, 2 × 2 factorial analysis: (1) High versus low hostile actor-clients by high versus low aggression tolerance aides, and (2) High versus low dependent actor-clients by high versus low dependency tolerance aides
Results: In progress.

Sutton, K. *Effects of modeled empathy and structured social class upon level of therapist displayed empathy.* Unpublished masters thesis, Syracuse University, 1970.
Trainees: Attendants (N = 60)
Skill: Empathy
Experimental design: High versus Low modeled empathy on immediate but not generalization measurement.
Results: No significant social class structuring or interaction effects.

Sutton-Simon, K. *The effects of two types of modeling and rehearsal procedures upon schizophrenics' social skill behavior.* Unpublished doctoral dissertation, Syracuse University, 1974.
Trainees: Psychiatric inpatients (N = 83, all male, all schizophrenic)
Skill: Social interaction behaviors
Experimental design: (1) SL with behavioral and cognitive models, (2) SL with behavioral models, (3) SL with cognitive models, (4) Attention control, (5) No-treatment control
Results: No significant between-condition differences.

Swanstrom, C. R. *An examination of Structured Learning Therapy and the helper therapy principle in teaching a self-control strategy to school children with conduct problems.* Unpublished doctoral dissertation, Syracuse University, 1978.
Trainees: Elementary school children with acting-out problems (N = 41, 30 boys, 11 girls)
Skill: Self-control
Experimental design: SL versus structured discussion by helper experience versus helper structuring versus no helper role plus brief instructions control
Results: SL and structured discussion significantly > control on self-control on acquisition. No significant transfer or helper role effects.

Trief, P. *The reduction of egocentrism in acting-out adolescents by Structured Learning Therapy.* Unpublished doctoral dissertation, Syracuse University, 1977.
Trainees: Adolescent boys with history of acting-out behaviors (N = 58)
Skill: Perspective-taking; cooperation
Experimental design: Presence versus Absence of SL for affective perspective taking by Presence versus Absence of SL for cognitive perspective taking plus No-treatment control
Results: All SL groups significantly > controls on perspective taking on acquisition. SL plus both affective and cognitive perspective-taking training significantly > controls on generalization criteria.

Walsh, W. G. *The effects of conformity pressure and modeling on the attraction of hospitalized patients toward an interviewer.* Unpublished doctoral dissertation, Syracuse University, 1971.
Trainees: Psychiatric inpatients (N = 60, all female, mostly schizophrenic)
Skill: Attraction
Experimental design: Presence versus Absence of high attraction modeling by Presence versus Absence of high attraction conformity pressure plus No-treatment control
Results: Significant main and interaction effects for modeling and conformity pressure on attraction. No significant generalization effect.

Wood, M. A. *Acquisition and transfer of assertiveness in passive and aggressive adolescents through the use of Structured Learning Therapy.* Unpublished doctoral dissertation, Syracuse University, 1977.
Trainees: Ninth grade students (N = 74)
Skill: Assertiveness
Experimental design: SL led by (1) teacher, (2) parent, or (3) student trainers by (1) passive or (2) aggressive trainees plus brief instructions control
Results: All SL groups significantly > control on assertiveness on acquisition and transfer criteria. SL-teacher trainer > SL-student trainer > SL-parent trainer on acquisition and minimal transfer criteria.

References

Abikoff, H., Gittelman-Klein, R., & Klein, D.F. Validation of a classroom observation code for hyperactive children. *Journal of Consulting and Clinical Psychology*, 1977, *45*, 772-783.

Abudabbah, N., Prandoni, J., & Jensen, D. Application of behavior principles to group therapy techniques with juvenile delinquents. *Psychological Reports*, 1972, *31*, 375-380.

Achenbach, T.M. The classification of children's psychiatric symptoms: A factor-analytic study. *Psychological Monographs*, 1966, *80* (Whole No. 615).

———. *Developmental psychopathology*. New York: Ronald Press, 1974.

Achenbach, T.M., & Edelbrock, C.S. The classification of child psychopathology: A review and analysis of empirical efforts. *Psychological Bulletin*, 1978, *85*, 1275-1301.

Adams, S. *Assessment of the psychiatric treatment program, phase I: Third interim report* (Research Report No. 21). Sacramento, Calif.: California Youth Authority, 1961.

———. The PICO project. In N. Johnston, L. Savitz, & M.E. Wolfgang (Eds.), *The Sociology of Punishment and Correction*. New York: Wiley, 1962.

Andrews, H.B. The systematic use of the Premack Principle in modifying classroom behaviors. *Child Study Journal*, 1970-1971, *1*, 74-79.

Arbuthnot, J. Modification of moral judgment through role playing. *Developmental Psychology*, 1975, *11*, 319-324.

Arkowitz, H., Lichtenstein, K.M., & Hines, P. The behavioral assessment of social competence in males. *Behavior Therapy*, 1975, *6*, 3-13.

Assagioli, R. *Psychosynthesis*. New York: Viking Press, 1965.

Authier, J., Gustafson, K., Guerney, B.G., Jr., & Kasdorf, J.A. The psychological practitioner as teacher. *The Counseling Psychologist*, 1975, *5*, 1-21.

Axelrod, S. Comparison of individual and group contingencies in two special classes. *Behavior Therapy*, 1973, *4*, 83-90.

Bailey, J.S., Wolf, M.M., & Phillips, E.L. Home-based reinforcement and the modification of pre-delinquents' classroom behavior. *Journal of Applied Behavior Analysis*, 1970, *3*, 223-233.

Bailey, W. *Correctional outcome: An evaluation of 100 reports.* Unpublished manuscript, University of California at Los Angeles, 1966.

Bandura, A. *Principles of behavior modification.* New York: Holt, Rinehart & Winston, 1969.

———. *Aggression: A social learning analysis.* Englewood Cliffs, N.J.: Prentice-Hall, 1973.

Bandura, A., Blanchard, E.B., & Ritter, B. The relative efficacy of desensitization and modeling approaches for inducing behavioral, affective and attitudinal changes. *Journal of Personality and Social Psychology,* 1969, *13,* 173-199.

Bandura, A., Grusec, J.E., & Manlove, F.L. Vicarious extinction of avoidance behavior. *Journal of Personality and Social Psychology,* 1967, *5,* 16-23.

Bandura, A., & Perloff, B. Relative efficacy of self-monitored and externally imposed reinforcement systems. *Journal of Personality and Social Psychology,* 1967, *7,* 111-116.

Bandura, A., Ross, D., & Ross, S.A. Transmission of aggression through imitation of aggressive models. *Journal of Abnormal and Social Psychology,* 1961, *63,* 575-582.

Bayh, B. *Our nation's schools—A report card: "A" in school violence and vandalism* (Preliminary report of the subcommittee to investigate juvenile delinquency. Committee on the Judiciary, United States Senate). Washington, D.C.: U.S. Government Printing Office, 1975.

Becker, W.C., Madsen, C.H., Arnold, C.R., & Thomas, D.R. The contingent use of teacher attention and praising in reducing classroom behavior problems. *Journal of Special Education,* 1967, *1,* 287-307.

Berlin, R.J. *Teaching acting-out adolescents prosocial conflict resolution through structured learning training of empathy.* Unpublished doctoral dissertation, Syracuse University, 1976.

Bernal, M.E., Duryee, J.S., Pruett, H.L., & Burns, B.J. Behavior modification and the brat syndrome. *Journal of Consulting and Clinical Psychology,* 1968, *32,* 447-456.

Blackham, G.J., & Silberman, A. *Modification of child and adolescent behavior.* New York: Wadsworth, 1975.

Bradford, L.P., Gibb, J.R., & Benne, K.R. *T-group theory and laboratory method.* New York: Wiley, 1964.

Brady, R.C. *Effects of success and failure on impulsivity and distractibility of three types of educationally handicapped children.* Unpublished doctoral dissertation, University of Southern California, 1970.

Braukmann, C.L., & Fixsen, D.L. Behavior modification with delinquents. In M. Herson, R.M. Eisler, & P.M. Miller (Eds.), *Progress in behavior modification.* New York: Academic Press, 1976.

Brehm, J.W., & Cohen, A.R. *Explorations in cognitive dissonance.* New York: Wiley, 1962.

Brock, T.C., & Blackwood, J.E. Dissonance reduction, social comparison, and modification of others' opinions. *Journal of Abnormal and Social Psychology,* 1962, *65,* 319-324.

Bryan, J.H., & Test, M.A. Models and helping: Naturalistic studies in aiding behavior. *Journal of Personality and Social Psychology,* 1967, 6, 400-407.

Burrs, V., & Kapche, R. *Modeling of social behavior in chronic hospital patients.* Unpublished manuscript, California State College at Long Beach, 1969.

California Department of the Youth Authority. *James Marshall treatment program: Progress report.* Sacramento, Calif.: California Youth Authority, 1967.

Callantine, M.F., & Warren, L.M. Learning sets in human concept formation. *Psychological Reports,* 1955, 1, 363-367.

Canale, J.R. The effect of modeling and length of ownership on sharing behavior of children. *Social Behavior and Personality,* 1977, 5, 187-191.

Carlsmith, J.M., Collins, B.E., & Helmreich, R.K. Studies in forced compliance: I. The effect of pressure for compliance on attitude change produced by face-to-face role playing and anonymous essay writing. *Journal of Personality and Social Psychology,* 1966, 4, 1-13.

Carney, F.J. *Summary of studies on the derivation of base expectancy categories for predicting recidivism of subjects released from institutions of the Massachusetts Department of Corrections.* Boston: Massachusetts Department of Corrections, 1966.

Castillo, G. *Left-handed teaching.* New York: Praeger, 1974.

Chapman, W.E. *Roots of character education.* Schenectedy, N.Y.: Character Research Press, 1977.

Chesler, M., & Fox, R. *Role playing methods in the classroom.* Chicago: Science Research Associates, 1966.

Chittenden, G.E. An experimental study in measuring and modifying assertive behavior in young children. *Monographs of the Society for Research in Child Development,* 1942, 7 (31).

Cobb, J.A., & Ray, R.S. The classroom behavioral observation code. In E.J. Mash & L.G. Terdal (Eds.), *Behavior therapy assessment: Diagnosis, design and evaluation.* New York: Springfield, 1976.

Craft, M., Stephenson, G., & Granger, C. A controlled trial of authoritarian and self-governing regimes with adolescent psychopaths. *American Journal of Orthopsychiatry,* 1964, 34, 543-554.

Cronbach, L.J., & Snow, R.E. *Aptitudes and instructional methods.* New York: Irvington Publishers, 1977.

Davis, K., & Jones, E.E. Changes in interpersonal perception as a means of reducing cognitive dissonance. *Journal of Abnormal and Social Psychology,* 1960, 61, 402-410.

Davidson, W.S., II, & Seidman, E. Studies of behavior modification and juvenile delinquency: A review, methodological critique, and social perspective. *Psychological Bulletin,* 1974, 8, 998-1011.

Davis, K., & Jones, E.E. Changes in interpersonal perception as a means of reducing cognitive dissonance. *Journal of Abnormal and Social Psychology,* 1960, 61, 402-410.

Dewey, J. *Experience and education.* New York: Collier, 1938.

Doke, L.A. Assessment of children's behavioral deficits. In M. Hersen & A.S. Bellack (Eds.), *Behavioral assessment: A practical handbook.* New York: Pergamon Press, 1976.

Drabman, R.S., Spitalnik, R., & O'Leary, K.D. Teaching self-control to disruptive children. *Journal of Abnormal Psychology,* 1973, *82,* 10-16.

Dreger, R.M., Lewis, P.M., Rich, T.A., Miller, K.S., Reid, M.P., Overlade, D.C., Taffel, C., & Flemming, E.L. Behavioral classification project. *Journal of Consulting Psychology,* 1964, *28,* 1-13.

Duncan, C.P. Transfer after training with single versus multiple tasks. *Journal of Experimental Psychology,* 1958, *55,* 63-73.

Eisler, R.M. The behavioral assessment of social skills. In M. Hersen & A.S. Bellack (Eds.), *Behavioral assessment: A practical handbook.* New York: Pergamon Press, 1976.

Eisler, R.M., Hersen, M., & Agras, W.S. Videotape: A method for the controlled observation of nonverbal interpersonal behavior. *Behavior Therapy,* 1973, *4,* 420-425.

Empey, L.T. Contemporary programs for convicted juvenile offenders: Problems of theory, practice and research. In D.J. Mulvihill & M.M. Tumin (Eds.), *Crimes of Violence* (Vol. 13). Washington, D.C.: U.S. Government Printing Office, 1969.

Empey, L.T., & Erikson, M.L. *The Provo experiment: Evaluating community control of delinquency.* Lexington, Mass.: Lexington Books, 1972.

Empey, L.T., & Lubeck, S.G. *The Silverlake experiment: Testing delinquency theory and community intervention.* Chicago: Aldine, 1971.

Evers, W.L., & Schwarz, J.C. Modifying social withdrawal in preschoolers: The effects of filmed modeling and teacher praise. *Journal of Abnormal Child Psychology,* 1973, *1,* 248-256.

Fairchild, L., & Erwin, W.M. Physical punishment by parent figures as a model of aggressive behavior in children. *Journal of Genetic Psychology,* 1977, *130,* 279-284.

Feshback, S. The function of aggression and the regulation of aggressive drive. *Psychological Review,* 1964, *71,* 247-272.

Friedenberg, W.P. *Verbal and non-verbal attraction modeling in an initial therapy interview analogue.* Unpublished masters thesis, Syracuse University, 1971.

Gardner, W.J. *Children with learning and behavior problems: A behavior management approach.* Boston: Allyn & Bacon, 1974.

Garrity, D. *The effects of length of incarceration upon parole adjustment and estimation of optimum sentence.* Unpublished doctoral dissertation, University of Washington, 1956.

Givner, A., & Graubard, P.S. *A handbook of behavior modification for the classroom.* New York: Holt, Rinehart & Winston, 1974.

Glasgow, R.E., & Arkowitz, H. The behavioral assessment of male and female social competence in dyadic heterosexual interactions. *Behavior Therapy,* 1975, *6,* 488-498.

Goldstein, A.P. (Ed.). *Prescriptions for child mental health and education.* New York: Pergamon Press, 1978.

Goldstein, A.P., Cohen, R., Blake, G., & Walsh, W. The effects of modeling and social class structuring in paraprofessional psychotherapist training. *Journal of Nervous and Mental Diseases,* 1971, *153,* 47-56.

Goldstein, A.P., & Goodhart, A. The use of structured learning for empathy enhancement in paraprofessional psychotherapist training. *Journal of Community Psychology,* 1973, *1,* 168-173.

Goldstein, A.P., Heller, K., & Sechrest, L.B. *Psychotherapy and the psychology of behavior change.* New York: Wiley, 1966.

Goldstein, A.P., & Kanfer, F.H. *Maximizing treatment gains: Transfer enhancement in psychotherapy.* New York: Academic Press, 1979.

Goldstein, A.P., Sherman, M., Gershaw, N.J., Sprafkin, R.P., & Glick, B. Training aggressive adolescents in prosocial behavior. *Journal of Youth and Adolescence,* 1978, *7,* 73-92.

Goldstein, A.P., & Stein, N. *Prescriptive psychotherapies.* New York: Pergamon Press, 1976.

Group for the Advancement of Psychiatry. Psychopathological disorders in childhood: Theoretical considerations and a proposed classification (GAP Report No. 62). Washington, D.C.: American Psychiatric Association, 1966.

Gruber, R.P. Behavior therapy: Problems in generalization. *Behavior Therapy,* 1971, *2,* 361-368.

Grusec, J.E., Kuczynski, L., Rushton, J.P., & Simutis, Z.M. Modeling, direct instruction and attributions: Effects on altruism. *Developmental Psychology,* 1978, *14,* 51-57.

Hall, R.V., Lund, D., & Jackson, D. Effects of teacher attention on study behavior. *Journal of Applied Behavior Analysis,* 1968, *1,* 1-12.

Harrison, R.M., & Mueller, P. Clue hunting about group counseling and parole outcome. Sacramento, Calif.: California Department of Corrections, 1964.

Hersen, M., & Bellack, A.S. (Eds.), *Behavioral assessment: A practical handbook.* New York: Pergamon Press, 1976.

Hewitt, L.E., & Jenkins, R.L. *Fundamental patterns of maladjustment: The dynamics of their origin.* Springfield, Ill.: State of Illinois, 1946.

Hollander, T.G. *The effects of role playing on attraction, disclosure and attitude change in a psychotherapy analogue.* Unpublished doctoral dissertation, Syracuse University, 1970.

Hubbel, A. Two person role playing for guidance in social readjustment. *Group Psychotherapy,* 1954, *7,* 249-254.

Hunt, D.E. *Matching models in education: The coordination of teaching methods with student characteristics.* Toronto: Ontario Institution for Studies in Education, 1971.

Iannotti, R.J. Effect of role-taking experiences on role taking, empathy, altruism and aggression. *Developmental Psychology,* 1977, *13,* 274-281.

Janis, J.L., & Mann, L. Effectiveness of emotional role playing in modifying smoking habits and attitudes. *Journal of Experimental Research in Personality,* 1965, *1,* 84-90.

Jesness, C. Comparative effectiveness of behavior modification and transactional analysis programs for delinquents. *Journal of Consulting and Clinical Psychology,* 1975, *43,* 758-779.

———. When is a delinquent a delinquent? A Reply to Shark & Handal. *Journal of Consulting and Clinical Psychology,* 1977, *45,* 696-697.

Johnson, O.G. *Tests and measurements in child development: Handbook II, volume 2.* San Francisco: Jossey-Bass, 1976.

Jones, R.A. *Self-fulfilling prophecies.* Hillsdale, N.J.: Erlbaum, 1977.

Kantor, J., Walker, C.E., & Hays, L. A study of the usefulness of Lanyon's psychological screening inventory with adolescents. *Journal of Consulting and Clinical Psychology,* 1976, *44,* 313-316.

Kassenbaum, G., Ward, D., & Wilner, D. *Prison treatment and its outcome.* New York: Wiley, 1972.

Kaufman, J.M., Gordon, M.E., & Baker, A. Being imitated: Persistence of an effect. *Journal of Genetic Psychology,* 1978, *132,* 319-320.

Kazdin, A.E. *Behavior modification in applied settings.* Homewood, Ill.: Dorsey Press, 1975.

Keller, M.F., & Carlson, P.M. The use of symbolic modeling to promote social skills in preschool children with low levels of social responsiveness. *Child Development,* 1974, *45,* 912-919.

Kent, R.N., & O'Leary, K.D. A controlled evaluation of behavior modification with conduct problem children. *Journal of Consulting and Clinical Psychology,* 1976, *44,* 586-596.

Kirkland, K.D., & Thelen, M.H. Uses of modeling in child treatment. In B.B. Lahey and A.E. Kazdin (Eds.), *Advances in Clinical Child Psychology.* New York: Plenum Press, 1977.

Klausmeier, H.J., Rossmiller, R.A., & Saily, M. (Eds.). *Individually guided elementary education.* New York: Academic Press, 1977.

Kleinsasser, L.D. *The reduction of performance anxiety as a function of desensitization, pre-therapy vicarious learning, and vicarious learning alone.* Unpublished doctoral dissertation, Pennsylvania State University, 1968.

Klinger, B.I. Effect of peer model responsiveness and length of induction procedure on hypnotic responsiveness. *Journal of Abnormal Psychology,* 1970, *75,* 15-18.

Knight, D. The Marshall program: Assessment of a short-term institutional treatment program (Research Report 56). Sacramento, Calif.: Department of the Youth Authority, 1969.

Kohlberg, L. *Collected papers on moral development and moral education.* Cambridge, Mass.: Harvard Graduate School of Education, 1973.

Krumboltz, J.D., & Thoresen, C.E. The effect of behavioral counseling in group and individual settings on information seeking behavior. *Journal of Counseling Psychology,* 1964, *11,* 324-333.

Krumboltz, J.D., Varenhorst, B.B., & Thoresen, C.E. Non-verbal factors in the effectiveness of models in counseling. *Journal of Counseling Psychology*, 1967, *14*, 412-418.

Kubany, E.S., & Sloggett, B.B. Coding Procedure for Teachers. In E.J. Mash & L.G. Terdal (Eds.), *Behavior therapy assessment: Diagnosis, design and evaluation*. New York: Springfield, 1976.

Lack, D.Z. *The effects of a model and instructions on psychotherapist self-disclosure*. Unpublished masters thesis, Syracuse University, 1971.

Lefkowitz, M., Blake, R.R., & Mouton, J.S. Status factors in pedestrian violation of traffic signals. *Journal of Abnormal and Social Psychology*, 1954, *51*, 704-706.

Lewinsohn, P.M. Manual of instructions for the behavioral ratings used for the observation of interpersonal behavior. In E.J. Mash & L.G. Terdal (Eds.), *Behavior therapy assessment: Diagnosis, design and evaluation*. New York: Springfield, 1976.

Liberman, B. *The effect of modeling procedures on attraction and disclosure in a psychotherapy analogue*. Unpublished doctoral dissertation, Syracuse University, 1970.

Lichtenstein, E., Keutzer, C.S., & Himes, K.H. Emotional role playing and changes in smoking attitudes and behaviors. *Psychological Reports*, 1969, *23*, 379-387.

Lipinski, D., & Nelson, R. Problems in the use of naturalistic observation as a means of behavioral assessment. *Behavior Therapy*, 1974, *5*, 341-351.

Litwak, S.E. *The use of the helper therapy principle to increase therapeutic effectiveness and reduce therapeutic resistance: Structured Learning Therapy with resistant adolescents*. Unpublished doctoral dissertation, Syracuse University, 1977.

Lowe, M.L., & Cuvo, A.J. Teaching coin summation to the mentally retarded. *Journal of Applied Behavior Analysis*, 1976, *9*, 483-489.

Madsen, C.H., Becker, W.C., & Thomas, D.R. Rules, praise and ignoring: Elementary classroom control. *Journal of Applied Behavior Analysis*, 1968, *1*, 139-150.

Mann, J.H. Experimental evaluations of role playing. *Psychological Bulletin*, 1956, *53*, 227-234.

Mann, R.A. Assessment of behavioral excesses in children. In M. Hersen & A.S. Bellack (Eds.), *Behavioral assessment. A practical handbook*. New York: Pergamon Press, 1972.

Manster, G.J. *Adolescent development and the life tasks*. Boston: Allyn & Bacon, 1977.

Marlatt, G.A., Jacobson, E.A., Johnson, D.L., & Morrice, D.J. Effect of exposure to a model receiving evaluative feedback upon subsequent behavior in an interview. *Journal of Consulting and Clinical Psychology*, 1970, *34*, 194-212.

Martinson, R. What works? Questions and answers about prison reform. *The Public Interest*, Spring 1974, 22-54.

Mash, E.J., & McElwee, J.D. Manual for coding interviews. In E.J. Mash & L.G. Terdal (Eds.), *Behavior therapy assessment: Diagnosis, design and evaluation.* New York: Springfield, 1976.

Mash, E.J., & Terdal, L.G. (Eds.), *Behavior therapy assessment: Diagnosis, design and evaluation.* New York: Springfield, 1976.

Matarazzo, J.D., Wiens, A.N., & Saslow, G. Studies in interview speech behavior. In L. Krasner & L.P. Ullman (Eds.), *Research in behavior modification.* New York: Holt, Rinehart and Winston, 1965.

Mately, R.E., & Acksen, B.A. The effect of role playing discrepant positions on change in moral judgments and attitudes. *Journal of Genetic Psychology,* 1976, *128,* 189-200.

McClintock, F. *Attendance centres.* London: Macmillan, 1961.

McCorkle, L., Elias, A., & Bixby, F. *The Highfields story: A unique experiment in the treatment of juvenile delinquency.* New York: Holt, 1958.

McFall, R.M., & Marston, A.R. An experimental investigation of behavior rehearsal in assertive training. *Journal of Abnormal Psychology,* 1970, *76,* 295-303.

McGehee, N., & Thayer, P.W. *Training in business and industry.* New York: Wiley, 1961.

McPhail, P., Ungold-Thomas, J., & Chapman, H. *Learning to care.* Niles, Ill.: Argus Communications, 1975.

Medland, M.B., & Stachnik, T.J. Good-behavior game: A replication and systematic analysis. *Journal of Applied Behavior Analysis,* 1972, *5,* 45-51.

Meichenbaum, D. Cognitive factors in behavior modification: Modifying what clients say to themselves. In R.D. Rubin, J.P. Brady, & J.D. Henderson (Eds.), *Advances in behavior therapy* (Vol. 4). New York: Academic Press, 1973.

Miller, J.P. *Humanizing the classroom.* New York: Praeger, 1976.

Nichols, H. Role playing in primary grades. *Group Psychotherapy,* 1954, *7,* 238-241.

Nolan, P.S., Kunzelmann, H.P., & Haring, N.G. Behavioral modification in a junior high learning disabilities classroom. *Exceptional Children,* 1967, *34,* 163-168.

O'Connor, R.D. Relative efficacy of modeling, shaping, and the combined procedures for modification of social withdrawal. *Journal of Abnormal Psychology,* 1972, *79,* 327-334.

Palmer, T.B. Matching worker and client in corrections. *Social Work,* 1973, *18,* 95-103.

————. The youth authority's community treatment project. *Federal Probation,* 1974, *38,* 3-14.

————. Martinson revisited. *Journal of Research in Crime and Delinquency,* July 1975, 133-152.

————. Final report to the California Community Treatment Project. Sacramento, Calif.: California Youth Authority, 1976.

Patterson, G.R. *The peer group as delinquency reinforcement agent.* Unpublished research report, Child Research Laboratory, University of Oregon, 1963.

Patterson, G.R., & Anderson, D. Peers as social reinforcers. *Child Development,* 1964, *35,* 951-960.

Patterson, G.R., & Gullion, M.E. *Living with children.* Champaign, Ill.: Research Press, 1972.

Patterson, G.R., Hops, H., & Weiss, R.L. Interpersonal skills training for couples in early stages of conflict. *Journal of Marriage and Family,* 1975, *37,* 295-301.

Patterson, G.R., McNeal, S., Hawkins, N., & Phelps, R. Reprogramming the social environment. *Journal of Child Psychology and Psychiatry,* 1967, *8,* 181-195.

Patterson, G.R., & Reid, J.B. Intervention for families of aggressive boys: A replication study. *Behavior Research & Therapy,* 1973, *11,* 383-394.

Perry, M.A. *Didactic instructions for and modeling of empathy.* Unpublished doctoral dissertation, Syracuse University, 1970.

Peterson, D.R., Quay, H.C., & Cameron, G.R. Personality and background factors in juvenile delinquency as inferred from questionnaire responses. *Journal of Consulting Psychology,* 1959, *23,* 392-399.

Peterson, D.R., Quay, H.C., & Tiffany, T.L. Personality factors related to juvenile delinquency. *Child Development,* 1961, *32,* 355-372.

Philips, E.L., Wolf, M.M., Fixen, D.L., & Bailey, J.S. The achievement place model: A community-based, family style, behavior modification program for predelinquents. In J.L. Khanna (Ed.), *New treatment approaches to juvenile delinquency.* Springfield, Ill.: Charles C. Thomas, 1975.

Pitkanen, L. The effect of simulation exercises on the control of aggressive behavior in children. *Scandinavian Journal of Psychology,* 1974, *15,* 169-177.

Quay, H.C. Dimensions of personality in delinquent boys as inferred from the factor analysis of case history data. *Child Development,* 1964, *35,* 479-484.

————. *Juvenile delinquency.* Princeton, N.J.: Van Nostrand, 1965.

————. Personality patterns in pre-adolescent delinquent boys. *Educational Psychological Measurement,* 1966, *26,* 99-110.

————. Patterns of aggression, withdrawal and immaturity. In H.C. Quay and J.S. Werry (Eds.), *Psychopathological disorders of childhood.* New York: Wiley, 1966.

Quay, H.C., & Quay, L.C. Behavior problems in early adolescence. *Child Development,* 1965, *36,* 215-220.

Rathjen, D., Hiniker, A., & Rathjen, E. *Incorporation of behavioral techniques in a game format to teach children social skills.* Paper presented at the meeting of the Association for Advancement of Behavior Therapy, New York, 1976.

Ray, R.S. Naturalistic assessment in educational settings: The classroom behavior observation code. In E.J. Mash & L.G. Terdal (Eds.), *Behavior therapy assess-*

ment: Diagnosis, design and evaluation. New York: Springer, 1976, pp. 279-285.

Richardson, C., & Meyer, R.C. Techniques in guided group interaction programs. *Child Welfare,* 1972, *51,* 519-527.

Ritter, B. Treatment of acrophobia with contact desensitization. *Behavior Research and Therapy,* 1969, *7,* 41-45.

Robinson, J., & Smith, G. The effectiveness of correctional programs. In R. Giallombardo (Ed.), *Juvenile Delinquency.* New York: Wiley, 1976.

Rogers-Warren, A., & Baer, D.M. Correspondence between saying and doing: Teaching children to share and praise. *Journal of Applied Behavior Analysis,* 1976, *9,* 335-354.

Rosenbaum, M.D., & Tucker, I.F. The competence of the model and the learning of imitation and non-imitation. *Journal of Experimental Psychology,* 1962, *63,* 183-190.

Rosenthal, T.L. Modeling therapies. In M. Hersen, R.M. Eisler, and P.M. Miller (Eds.), *Progress in behavior modification* (Vol. 2). New York: Academic Press, 1976.

Ross, A.O., Lacey, H.M., & Parton, D.A. The development of a behavior checklist for boys. *Child Development,* 1965, *36,* 1013-1027.

Ross, D.M., Ross, S.A., & Evans, T.A. The modification of extreme social withdrawal by modeling with guided participation. *Journal of Behavior Therapy and Experimental Psychiatry,* 1976, *2,* 273-279.

Ryan, A.J., & Hoffman, T. *Social studies and the child's expanding self.* New York: Intext Press, 1973.

Sealy, A., & Banks, C. Social maturity, training, experience and recidivism amongst British borstal boys. *British Journal of Criminology,* 1971, *11,* 245-264.

Seckel, J.P. The Freemont experiment: Assessment of residential treatment at a youth authority reception center. Sacramento, Calif.: California Department of Youth Authority, 1967.

Shark, M., & Handal, P.J. Reliability and validity of the Jesness Inventory: A caution. *Journal of Consulting and Clinical Psychology,* 1977, *45,* 692-695.

Shoabs, N.E. Role playing in the individual psychotherapy interview. *Journal of Individual Psychology,* 1964, *26,* 84-89.

Shore, E., & Sechrest, L. Concept attainment as a function of number of positive instances presented. *Journal of Educational Psychology,* 1961, *52,* 303-307.

Simon, S.B., Howe, L.W., & Kirschenbaum, H. *Values clarification.* New York: Hart, 1972.

Slavson, S.R. *A textbook in analytic group psychotherapy.* New York: International Universities Press, 1964.

Sloane, H.N. *Classroom management: Remediation and prevention.* New York: Wiley, 1976.

Solomon, R.W., & Wahler, R.G. Peer reinforcement control of classroom problem behavior. *Journal of Applied Behavior Analysis,* 1973, *6,* 49-56.

Spivack, G., & Shure, M. *Social adjustment of young children.* San Francisco: Jossey-Bass, 1974.

Staub, E. The use of role playing and induction in children's learning of helping and sharing behavior. *Child Development,* 1971, *42,* 805-816.

Staub, E. The learning and unlearning of aggression. In J. Singer (Ed.), *The control of aggression and violence.* New York: Academic Press, 1971.

Stein, N., & Bogin, D. Individual child psychotherapy. In A.P. Goldstein (Ed.). *Prescriptions for child mental health and education.* New York: Pergamon Press, 1978.

Stram, P.S., Cooke, T.P., & Apolloni, T. The role of peers in modifying classmates social behavior: A review. *Journal of Special Education,* 1976, *10,* 351-356.

Stumphauser, J.S. Increased delay of gratification in young prison inmates through imitation of high-delay peer models. *Journal of Personality and Social Psychology,* 1972, *21,* 10-17.

Sullivan, H.S. *Conceptions of modern psychiatry.* New York: Norton, 1953.

Sutton, K. *Effects of modeled empathy and structured social class upon level of therapist displayed empathy.* Unpublished masters thesis, Syracuse University, 1970.

Thelen, M.H., Fry, R.A., Dollinger, S., Jr., & Smith, S.C. Use of videotaped models to improve the interpersonal adjustment of delinquents. *Journal of Consulting and Clinical Psychology,* 1976, *44,* 492.

Toner, I.J., Moore, L.P., & Ashley, P.K. The effect of serving as a model of self-control on subsequent resistance to deviation in children. *Journal of Experimental Child Psychology,* 1978, *26,* 85-91.

Tsoi, M.M., & Yule, W. The effects of group reinforcement in classroom behavior modification. *Educational Studies,* 1976, *2,* 129-140.

Turkat, J.D., & Feuerstein, M. Behavior modification and the public misconception. *American Psychologist,* 1978, *33,* 194-197.

Tyler, V.O., & Brown, G.D. Token reinforcement of academic performance with institutionalized delinquent boys. *Journal of Educational Psychology,* 1968, *59,* 164-168.

Vinter, R., & Janowitz, M. Effective institutions for juvenile delinquents: A research statement. *Social Service Review,* 1959, *33,* 118-130.

Vorrath, H.H., & Brendtro, L.K. *Positive peer culture.* Chicago: Aldine, 1974.

Wahler, R.G. Setting generality: Some specific and general effects of child behavior therapy. *Journal of Applied Behavior Analysis,* 1969, *2,* 239-246.

Walker, H.M., & Buckley, N.K. Programming generalization and maintenance of treatment effects across time and across settings. *Journal of Applied Behavior Analysis,* 1972, *5,* 209-224.

Walsh, W. *The effects of conformity pressure and modeling on the attraction of hospitalized patients toward an interviewer.* Unpublished doctoral dissertation, Syracuse University, 1971.

Warren, M.Q. The community treatment project: History and prospects. In S.A. Yefsky (Ed.), *Law enforcement science and technology.* London: Academic Press, 1967.

Warren, M.Q. *Classification for treatment.* Paper presented at Seminar on the Classification of Criminal Behavior held by the National Institute of Law Enforcement and Criminal Justice, Washington, D.C., 1974.

Weinstein, G., & Fantini, M.D. *Toward humanizing education: A curriculum of affect.* New York: Praeger, 1970.

Yates, A. (Ed.). *Grouping in education.* New York: Wiley, 1966.

Zimmerman, B.J., & Dialissi, F. Modeling influences on children's creative behavior. *Journal of Educational Psychology,* 1973, *65,* 127-134.

INDEX

About the Authors

ARNOLD P. GOLDSTEIN earned his Ph.D. at Pennsylvania State University. He has worked at the University of Pittsburgh Medical School, the VA Outpatient Research Laboratory in Washington, D.C., and at Syracuse University since 1963. He is a Professor of Psychology there and Director of the University Counseling and Psychotherapy Center. His career-long concern, both as a researcher and clinician, has been enhancing the effectiveness of psychotherapy. Dr. Goldstein is the author or editor of 18 books and over 60 articles dealing with active therapeutic ingredients, research methods, behavior change procedures, aggression control, and the teaching of prosocial skills. His books include: *Therapist-Patient Expectancies in Psychotherapy; Psychotherapy and the Psychology of Behavior Change; Psychotherapeutic Attraction; The Lonely Teacher; Police Crisis Intervention; Hostage; Structured Learning Therapy;* and *Skill Training for Community Living.*

ROBERT P. SPRAFKIN earned his A.B. at Dartmouth College, his M.A. and Professional Diploma at Columbia University Teachers College, and his Ph.D. at Ohio State University. He was a member of the psychology faculty of Syracuse University from 1968-1971. Currently he directs the Day Treatment Center for the Syracuse Veterans Administration Hospital and holds academic ranks of Adjunct Associate Professor of Psychology at Syracuse University and Clinical Assistant Professor of Psychiatry at the State University of New York, Upstate Medical Center. He is co-editor of the book *Working with Police Agencies* and co-author (with Goldstein and

Gershaw) of *Skill Training for Community Living: Applying Structured Learning Therapy* and *I Know What's Wrong but I Don't Know What to Do About It.* He has also authored numerous articles for professional journals dealing with psychological treatments, program evaluation, and training.

N. JANE GERSHAW earned her Ph.D. from Syracuse University. She is a clinical psychologist who has worked at Norristown State Hospital and Hahnemann Medical College and Community Mental Health Center, and she currently practices at the Syracuse Veterans Administration Mental Hygiene Clinic. She holds adjunct faculty appointments of Assistant Professor of Psychology at Syracuse University and Clinical Assistant Professor of Psychiatry at the State University of New York, Upstate Medical Center. Dr. Gershaw is engaged in the practice of psychotherapy, with special interest in therapeutic groups. She has been active in the training of professional and paraprofessional group psychotherapists and in the development of psychoeducational and group therapy techniques useful with a variety of psychiatric and nonpsychiatric populations. She is co-author, along with Drs. Sprafkin and Goldstein, of *Skill Training for Community Living* and *I Know What's Wrong but I Don't Know What to Do About It.*

PAUL KLEIN earned his A.B. at Colgate University and his M.A. at the State University of New York; he also has a New York State Special Education Teaching Certificate in the areas of emotional handicaps and learning disabilities. His career involvements have been in the areas of musical composition and performance, media production, and education. In music and media productions, he has composed the sound tracks for the C.I.N.E. Golden Eagle Award-winning animated film short, *Moments Spent,* animated by Gerald McDermott, and Bruce Cayard's animated short, *The Friendly Lion,* and performed and produced his own compositions and film sound track score (recorded by Capitol Records). In education, he has founded and co-directed an alternative school for severely emotionally disturbed students, taught junior high school students with emotional and behavior disorders, and conducted numerous workshops for teachers in the management of students with behavior disorders.